Counseling Children and Adolescents in Schools

Practice and Application Guide

Counseling Children and Adolescents in Schools

Practice and Application Guide

Sandy Magnuson

*Retired Counselor Educator and
Elementary School Counselor*

■

Robyn S. Hess

University of Northern Colorado

■

Linda Beeler

Capella University

Los Angeles | London | New Delhi
Singapore | Washington DC

Los Angeles | London | New Delhi
Singapore | Washington DC

FOR INFORMATION:

SAGE Publications, Inc.
2455 Teller Road
Thousand Oaks, California 91320
E-mail: order@sagepub.com

SAGE Publications Ltd.
1 Oliver's Yard
55 City Road
London EC1Y 1SP
United Kingdom

SAGE Publications India Pvt. Ltd.
B 1/I 1 Mohan Cooperative Industrial Area
Mathura Road, New Delhi 110 044
India

SAGE Publications Asia-Pacific Pte. Ltd.
33 Pekin Street #02-01
Far East Square
Singapore 048763

Printed in the United States of America

ISBN 9781412990882

Acquisitions Editor: Kassie Graves
Editorial Assistant: Courtney Munz
Production Editor: Astrid Virding
Copy Editor: Patricia Sutton
Typesetter: C&M Digitals (P) Ltd.
Proofreader: Dennis W. Webb
Cover Designer: Bryan Fishman
Marketing Manager: Katie Winter
Permissions Editor: Adele Hutchinson

Certified Chain of Custody
Promoting Sustainable Forestry
www.sfiprogram.org
SFI-01268

SUSTAINABLE FORESTRY INITIATIVE

SFI label applies to text stock

14 15 10 9 8 7 6 5 4 3 2

Introduction

Congratulations! You have purchased your tickets for an exciting journey on which you will learn about a fulfilling and rewarding career. School counselors and school psychologists have opportunities to make a difference in the lives of children and youth on a daily basis. As professional helpers in schools, we are delighted to share our experiences in these wonderful professions with you. We look forward to joining you on this portion of your career journey.

> Tour Guide Note of Explanation: This *Counseling Children and Adolescents in Schools: Practice and Application Guide* is a supplement and companion text for *Counseling Children and Adolescents in Schools*. We provide it as a bridge to connect theoretical frameworks and practical school situations. It is designed to assist as you learn basic counseling skills and when you begin applying basic skills during individual counseling sessions. In many school counseling and school psychology preparation programs, this experience is called *counseling practicum*; however, the courses in your program may have different sequences and course titles.
>
> Learning the practical applications of theoretical concepts is a career-long challenge; thus, we have used the journey metaphor. We view our roles as guides but not bosses! We hope that you view the companion texts, *Counseling Children and Adolescents in Schools* and this *Practice and Application Guide* (sometimes referred to as the *Guide*), as another set of resources—particularly as you prepare for and enter careers as school psychologists and school counselors. And now, back to the metaphoric tours we'll share.

Your itinerary for this portion of your journey, provided in Table 1.1, is somewhat flexible. Though we have presented our series of tours sequentially, your journey may not be linear. Your instructors, supervisors, and sojourners may recommend alternate routes, additional excursions, digressions, and layovers. The tours are designed with time flexibility as well. You may stroll through some and jog through others. You may find that a few of the tours are more arduous than others.

Table 1.1 Itinerary

Tour 1 Preparation for Departure: Who Am I and How Do I Interact With Others?

Reflective Practice: For Now, It *Is* All About You!

Exploring Your Own Beliefs

Giving and Receiving Feedback

Tour 2 Preparation for Departure: Building Relationships With Basic Listening Skills

Exploring Authenticity, Respect, Empathy, and Engagement

Counseling Relationship as the Essential Ingredient:
A Theoretical Review

Becoming Familiar With Basic Skills

Nonverbal Attending

Tracking

Paraphrasing

Reflecting Affect

Clarifying

Summarizing

Skillful Use of Questions

Pitfalls to Avoid

Before You Conduct Your First Session or a Session in an Unfamiliar Situation

Using Skills in Combination

Tour 3 Departure: Advanced Facilitation Skills

Empathy: Theory and Research

Immediacy

Self-Disclosure

Challenging

Interpretation

Reflecting Meaning

An unusual feature of this journey is the absence of a destination. This is not a round trip, although you may find that it is cyclical from time to time. You will also find that it is expansive rather than linear. In addition to having no destination, the journey does not have an exact departure place and time. Clearly the journey is yours. You are, ultimately, the captain. Toward the end of the tours in this *Guide* you will likely find that the scenery changes dramatically as you actually become an active contributor. That will be a signal that our participation as temporary guides on your journey has served its purpose, and we will bid you farewell.

At the beginning of several tours, we have provided orientation information, some of which will be a review for you. We will explore notions of authenticity, respect, empathy, and engagement. Rather than "packing" these concepts in preparation for departure, we will "unpack" them as we endeavor to make sense of them at various stops along the journey. Your luggage will expand as you attain new skills, new tools, and new ideas. As we move from one tour to the next, we will endeavor to carefully package acquisitions because you will use them throughout your journey.

Our responsibilities for accompanying you on this portion of your professional journey will near completion by the time we begin the fourth tour, when you assume more of a leadership role. Rather than "seeing new sites" you will encounter an invitation to make sense of the various tours for you, personally, and for your work as a professional school counselor or school psychologist. You will likely refer to previous travel resources, such as *Counseling Children and Adolescents in Schools*, as you tease out the relevance of theories and frameworks for your work as a school-based professional helper in schools. You will become more reflective in the process of determining how all the "sites" you have viewed on these and other tours of your journey coalesce into meaningful, internally consistent methods and models that fit for you.

As you participate in various activities in this *Counseling Children and Adolescents in Schools: Practice and Application Guide,* we hope you will personalize the exercises by visualizing a school environment in which you might work and by giving names and faces to students who are described. For example, you will be asked to write a response to a 9-year-old girl who says, "Whenever I have to take tests, my stomach starts to hurt. I'm so stupid and I hate tests!" Create a mental picture of this student. What does she look like? What color is her skin? What color is her hair? What is her name? Your pictures of the student will help you compose a more personal response.

We also hope you enjoy your interactions with the students we have included. They represent actual living, dynamic, precious young people with whom you will work during your practicum, during your internship, and throughout your career. We hope you are humbled, as we are, by the awesome privilege and responsibility that goes with being a school psychologist or school counselor.

Welcome aboard! Let's get started!

TOUR 1

Preparation for Departure

Who Am I and How Do I Interact With Others?

Learning Objectives

- Explore personal beliefs and values related to helping children and adolescents
- Understand the intra- and interpersonal skills necessary for successful work with students, their parents, and their teachers
- Consider ways to give and receive feedback
- Explore manifestations of cultural difference

The relationships you develop with students as well as adults will be central to your work in schools. As a school-based professional, you are a key component of those relationships with primary responsibility for building them. Throughout your preparation program, you will likely encounter invitations to examine your own thoughts, feelings, attitudes, and reactions—perhaps at deeper levels than you have previously explored. You may be asked to do so with your peers, your instructors, and your supervisors, which can be uncomfortable at first.

We often show only one part of ourselves in our professional and academic communities. Bringing our personal components to university settings may be unfamiliar, and it may produce discomfort. However, to become an effective helper, you must be willing to reflect, to consider the intention of your responses, and to continually challenge yourself to take personal risks to understand yourself as well as the student clients with whom you will work.

We encourage you to engage in a process of self-evaluation and self-monitoring now, and throughout your career, so you can continue to grow as a professional and a person.

It is important to identify your current beliefs about children and adolescents, your ideas about how people change, and your understanding of the context of schools.

REFLECTIVE PRACTICE: FOR NOW, IT *IS* ALL ABOUT YOU!

What do we mean by reflection and why is it so important? Literally, *self-reflection* means self-examination or introspection. It is intentional consideration of why we do the things we do. According to Schon (1987), we learn best through continuous action and reflection about everyday concerns in life. From his perspective, new professionals use a blend of knowledge, theory, and values to understand new situations that arise in practice. Over time, these components blend into personal theories that guide actions.

The reflective process brings these personal theories into awareness. Through active reflection, individuals entertain a "sorting" process during which aspects of personal and professional theories that seem sound are maintained, and those components without veracity are discarded. With time and experience, and through the process of reflection, practitioners begin to reliably and intentionally use their personal theories, in combination with established counseling approaches, when deciding on an appropriate course of action for novel situations. Thus, self-reflection is critical to professional growth and ongoing development.

Sometimes, as we move into demanding professional positions, we feel pressed for time and believe that self-reflection is no longer necessary. However, it is even more critical that we continue to evaluate our thoughts and actions as we continue to face the complex and challenging issues presented by students in school settings.

Self-reflection is not easily explained or taught. However, exercises such as small group discussion, journal writing, case analyses, and role play often facilitate reflection (Stickel & Trimmer, 1994). We encourage you to participate in these activities in order to develop the habit of continuous professional self-reflection.

In addition to participating in the guided reflection opportunities provided in this practice guide, in the accompanying textbook, and through your classes, we encourage you to maintain a reflective journal. After counseling sessions, you may achieve clarity as you journal your thoughts and feelings about the session in response to a sequence of questions: What's going on with you *right now*? What did you do well? When did you struggle? What do you wish you would have done differently? When did your personal experiences hinder *and* when did they help?

Your journal will also document your growth over time. As you periodically read your entries (e.g., every few weeks during an academic term, at the end of a term, after your first year), you will have additional opportunities to reflect on your growth and the areas in which you have been challenged.

Smyth (1989) recommended the following structure for analyzing professional development, particularly after role plays and counseling sessions, with a series of four questions related to one's work:

(a)   Describing: What do I do?

(b)   Informing: What does this mean?

(c) Confronting: How did I come to be like this?

(d) Reconstructing: How might I do things differently? (p. 2)

Through this type of synthesis, both new and experienced practitioners continually explore their own beliefs and the ways in which they impact their practice.

Preparing for Guided Reflection

Visit with your instructor or supervisor about his or her recommendations, preferences, and requirements regarding a journal. Some instructors invite a written dialogue as they periodically collect journals and respond to students' entries. Others regard the journals as students' private records.

1. Purchase a composition book, create a notebook, or create an electronic file for your journal.

2. Prepare a cover or title page. You may want to compose a title that personalizes your journal. For example, I (S.M.) titled one of my journals as *Sandy: From the Country to the Clinic. Practicum I, Summer 1982*.

3. Date the first or second blank page, and allow your thoughts and feelings about what you've read thus far to flow through your pen and on to the paper. If you cannot think of anything to write, begin by answering questions raised in the previous section. Try to avoid censoring or attempting to "look good."

EXPLORING YOUR OWN BELIEFS

One of the first areas to consider includes your personal beliefs about children and adolescents. Do you see children as weak and vulnerable beings who need to be protected? Are adolescents unpredictable and difficult? Your response to both of these questions may fluctuate among yes, no, and maybe.

What *do* I believe about kids?

As you build the theoretical foundation of your counseling practice, you should examine your beliefs not only about people in general but also about children as opposed to adults. One of the beliefs that I (R.S.H.) have encountered with graduate students is the idea that children don't really experience awful things in their lives or have anything "wrong" with them. This belief is likely related to their own comfortable childhood experiences as well as inexperience. Our generalized beliefs are often inaccurate or faulty.

When faulty beliefs are not challenged, preservice, as well as inservice, professionals are more likely to miss important information that students and adults directly or indirectly provide. For example, in some instances, children may not be able to directly share that they are being hurt. Instead, they may provide only hints or clues about their fear and pain. The faulty belief that "children don't experience problems" might result in the helper missing these important clues. Conversely, if you believe that all children are likely victims of abusive families, you may find yourself overreacting to a bruise on a child's arm.

Can people change?
How?!
What roles and tools do professional helpers hold in the process?

Your ideas about change and what helps people make changes are other areas to explore. Do people change only when given the tools? Do people have to figure out their own paths to change? Are people able to change? Can education be a transformational experience? Can school psychologists and school counselors do things to help children and youth make changes to improve their lives? We hope you answered *yes* to the last question. If you didn't, you may need to rethink your career path.

Regardless of your theoretical orientation, it is helpful if you believe that children and adolescents can change. By saying this, we are not implying that something is wrong with the young person sitting across from you, only that there is something in that individual's life that is contributing to a feeling of discomfort and unhappiness. The "change" may be facilitated by helping that young person develop a different perspective of the issue or a new strategy for coping with a difficult situation.

An additional area for exploration falls into the more nebulous areas of beliefs related to contemporary, value laden, controversial topics. Students in the schools often come from different socioeconomic, cultural, and religious backgrounds than your own. They may be questioning their sexual orientation, experimenting with drugs and alcohol, or engaging in premarital sex. They may harbor prejudice against minority populations or be members of gangs. How will you respond? How will your beliefs and values guide you? More important, how can you acknowledge your own beliefs and values yet not impose them on students?

What values do you hold that might interfere with your ability to form a therapeutic alliance with a student client?

I (S.M.) remember visiting a counselor who had decorated her office with Biblical quotes and praying hands on the wall. Further, a Bible was prominently displayed on her desk. When I mentioned the decor of the office to my preservice school counselors, they struggled with my concerns. They contended that she was simply "being herself." They thought authenticity was appropriate and important. They ultimately began to grapple with ways those symbols would affect the students who come to see her, especially if they didn't share similar beliefs. Over time, they were able to achieve objectivity as they considered the prominence of Christian symbols in the context of school counselors' ethical guidelines and values related to access, unconditional positive regard, and respect for all students.

Various instruments have been developed to help beginning practitioners think about their beliefs related to multicultural issues. For example, the Multicultural Awareness-Knowledge-Skills Survey ([MAKSS]; D'Andrea, Daniels, & Heck, 1991) is an instrument designed to gather information on the effect of different instructional strategies on improving the cultural awareness and sensitivity of preservice practitioners (although this self-assessment was published over 20 years ago, it is often referenced in current publications). There are many other informal instruments that also help pre- and inservice professionals think about their values and beliefs related to aspects of counseling such as silence and resistance.

GIVING AND RECEIVING FEEDBACK

As you explore your own beliefs and values, your peers in the class or group will be engaged in similar pursuits. Throughout your career, but particularly during graduate school, you will have many opportunities not only to grow personally and professionally, but also to support the growth of others. Many skills classes, practica, internships, and supervision groups are structured to include peer feedback as an important part of the learning process. You will likely engage in role plays with your peers and have opportunities to observe videotaped or live role plays as well as counseling sessions.

Giving feedback to peers can be difficult, and your inclination may be to refrain from giving any type of reaction or opinion that might be viewed as negative. Often preservice professionals believe that they are such novices at counseling that they don't have helpful comments to provide. On the contrary, preservice professionals appreciate the diverse perspectives of their peers. Every individual attends to different aspects of the observed session. Taken together, these insights create a more detailed and comprehensive picture of the developing professional's strengths and areas for growth.

As you consider the type of feedback to provide and the manner in which it is given, it is important to remember that the ultimate purpose is to facilitate continued growth. When feedback is provided with this intent, it is likely to be well received. We also provide these guidelines to assist you in giving your opinions and reactions to peer counseling sessions.

- Limit the amount of feedback given at any one time. It can be overwhelming to your peers. Select one or two key areas on which to focus.
- Be sure to note positive aspects of the session as well as areas for growth.
- In your feedback, be clear and descriptive. It is helpful if you can provide an example from the session that illustrates your point.
- When your feedback is corrective, provide an example of the type of behavior that could be used instead.
- Address behaviors that can be altered rather than personal attributes of an individual.

Not only will you provide feedback to your peers, but you will also be a recipient of this type of critique. It can be difficult to sit back and hear about the many aspects of your session that did not go the way you had hoped. A natural inclination is to defend and explain. Alternatively, you may feel discouraged by comments that you view as negative. Although it might be difficult at first, it is best to listen to the feedback with an open attitude. If you disagree, you do not need to share that with the person providing the feedback. Sometimes, it is helpful to write the comments you receive. Later, when you are watching your tape or meeting with your supervisor, you can decide whether you want to incorporate the suggestion into future sessions.

We encourage you to maintain the same mind-set as when you are providing feedback to others. The purpose of this information is to facilitate growth. As you come to trust your peers and your supervisor on this point, you will likely find that you request suggestions and strategies for improving your skills.

Complete the Multicultural Awareness-Knowledge-Skills Survey (D'Andrea et al., 1991) or a similar inventory.

1. What did you learn about yourself as you responded to the items on the inventory?

_____

_____

_____

_____

2. What surprised you?

_____

_____

_____

_____

_____

3. How can you broaden your experiences with diverse groups?

_____

_____

_____

_____

4. How can you enhance your knowledge, awareness, and skills?

_____

_____

_____

_____

_____

5. What personal attributes and abilities will be your assets as a professional helper in schools?

_____

_____

_____

_____

_____

6. Consider a time when you experienced significant personal growth. What was the impetus for the growth? What did you do to perpetuate and reinforce it?

_____

_____

_____

_____

_____

7. Consider your responses to crises in your life. How have you responded? What have you done to resolve the difficult time?

_____

_____

_____

_____

_____

8. For a moment or two, think about the counseling experiences you may have in the next few weeks and the requirements you must meet this term. What thoughts come to your mind?

_____

_____

_____

_____

_____

9. Imagine yourself providing individual counseling to a student and thinking, "Things are going well! This is working!" What are you doing and what is the student doing?

_____

_____

_____

_____

_____

10. Imagine that suddenly the student client becomes silent. How will that experience be for you?

_____

_____

_____

_____

_____

11. Imagine that the student does not wish to return for additional counseling after one or two sessions. How will that be for you?

_____

_____

_____

_____

_____

12. Try to create an image of a student client sitting in your office with you and your thoughts being, "Please! Not this!" Who is the student (e.g., in terms of age, gender, ethnicity, financial status, and so forth), and what is the issue or problem that this individual is presenting?

_____

_____

_____

_____

_____

13. Try to create an image of an adult in your office who evokes the same reaction. Who is the adult, and what prompted the interaction?

_____

_____

_____

_____

_____

14. As you examine and identify your personal spiritual, religious, and ethical values, list those that will contribute to your effectiveness as a professional helper and those that may interfere.

_____

_____

_____

_____

_____

TOUR 2

Preparation for Departure

Building Relationships With Basic Listening Skills

Learning Objectives

- Recognize the importance of a helping relationship
- Master basic listening skills
- Learn to ask questions that facilitate professional relationships and change
- Evaluate and improve professional helpers' responses
- Become aware of professional helpers' common mistakes

EXPLORING AUTHENTICITY, RESPECT, EMPATHY, AND ENGAGEMENT

In the third chapter of *Counseling Children and Adolescents in Schools*, we described a variety of developmental milestones children and youth experience. We also view learning and honing counseling skills as a developmental process. *Basic skills* (sometimes called core skills, or microskills) that are developed on this tour include (a) nonverbal attending, (b) tracking, (c) paraphrasing, (d) reflecting affect, (e) clarifying, (f) summarizing, and (g) skillful use of questions. These skills are, essentially, good communication strategies that help us develop relationships—personal, collegial, and professional.

Think about someone with whom you have had conversations during which you felt understood, accepted, and validated. What did or does that person do that enables you to think of him or her in this context?

_____

_____

_____

_____

_____

Typically, responses include such components as: (a) She looked at me, (b) he nodded, (c) his facial expressions let me know, (d) he said things so I knew he was listening, and (e) she stopped doing what she was doing and gave me her full attention. For children and adolescents, these verbal and nonverbal behaviors are much the same, although there may be slight differences in these interactions that help facilitate communication.

Think a bit further back in history to when you were a child or adolescent. Identify two or three adults with whom you could talk openly and feel understood. What were some of the reasons you identified these adults?

_____

_____

_____

_____

_____

Unfortunately, many children and youth do not have opportunities for relationships like you may have described. Thus, it is important for school counselors and school psychologists to offer a qualitatively different experience during which young people experience respect, unconditional positive regard, attention, and understanding.

COUNSELING RELATIONSHIP AS THE ESSENTIAL INGREDIENT: A THEORETICAL REVIEW

Sometimes practicing basic skills seems tedious, mechanical, and artificial. That being the case, we start with *why* to use them rather than *how* to use them. A variety of empirical studies have resulted in evidence regarding the importance of the counseling relationship (Lambert & Barley, 2001; Wampold, 2001). In fact, Lambert and

Barley (2001) contended, "It is imperative that clinicians remember that decades of research consistently demonstrate that relationship factors correlate more highly with client outcomes than do specialized treatment techniques" (p. 359). In some fields, this relationship is also referred to as the therapeutic alliance or allegiance. Regardless of the terminology, we believe that a strong working alliance with student clients is essential. The relationship process is as important with children and youth as it is with adults, and in schools as it is in community agencies.

Our professional histories reflect diverse beliefs regarding counseling relationships. For example, Freud's involvement with clients was equated with a blank screen. Nonetheless, transference and countertransference were rooted in the therapeutic relationship. The patient–psychiatrist relationship and the clinician's attentiveness were critically important. Freud's student, Adler, may have been the first to emphasize the importance of counseling relationships characterized by empathy and respect. Adlerian helpers' initial task is to facilitate a therapeutic relationship characterized by equality, mutual trust, respect, involvement, and confidence. Consistent with the broader theory, the provision of such a relationship contributes to students' socialization (Dreikurs, 1967).

Perhaps it was Carl Rogers who became the herald of the counseling relationship. According to Rogers (1961), the relationship is more than the foundation for counseling; the *relationship* is the therapy. In Rogers's words, "if I can provide a certain type of relationship, the other person will discover within himself or herself the capacity to use that relationship for growth and change, and personal development will occur" (p. 3). Rogers demonstrated his trust for others as he listened to them, cared about them, encouraged them, and facilitated egalitarian relationships with them (Bankart, 1997).

> Even though we emphasize the relationship, there are times when you'll need to focus on the presenting issue first (e.g., in cases of abuse, crisis intervention). Remain flexible in your approach.

In recent years, mental health professionals have recognized that the relationship is not the only necessary condition for growth to occur in some cases. Instead, a blend of the therapeutic relationship and the treatment method contribute to successful outcomes.

BECOMING FAMILIAR WITH BASIC SKILLS

Let's start with an experiment. We suggest doing this with another person. However, if you are alone, you can use a mirror.

1. With your partner, initiate a conversation during which you both cross your arms, cross your legs, lean back, and avoid eye contact. What happens?

2. For the second stage of the experiment, pretend that one of you is a school counselor and one of you is a middle school student. While the student tries to visit

with the counselor about college admissions procedures, the counselor should, once again, cross his or her legs and arms, lean back, and avoid eye contact. How is this for both of you?

3. Reverse roles, and repeat the second step.

4. For the final step in this experiment, take turns trying to communicate interest, attention, and concern without using any words. Again, give feedback to one another.

NONVERBAL ATTENDING

"One cannot not communicate" (Watzlawick, Beavin, & Jackson, 1967, p. 48) is a broadly accepted family systems principle. Whether or not we say a word, we transmit messages. These nonverbal messages are potent, even though they are quite vulnerable to misinterpretation. Nonverbal behaviors can be used to communicate (a) emotion, (b) changes in the interpersonal relationship between the professional and the student, (c) attitudes about oneself, and (d) discrepancies between one's internal state and verbal behavior (Highlen & Hill, 1984). For optimal clarity, then, professionals strive for congruence between verbal and nonverbal attending. We also remain alert to incongruent messages we receive.

Nonverbal communication, sometimes called *analog*, includes many factors. For example, our voice tones and variations contribute to messages. Posture, appearance, gestures, facial expressions, and even breathing are other elements of nonverbal communication. Generally, nonverbal attending skills include:

- Maintaining appropriate levels of eye contact
- Uncrossing arms and legs
- Leaning slightly forward
- Changing facial expressions and voice tones according to verbal communication
- Avoiding distracting mannerisms (e.g., twirling hair, waving hands in the air)
- Appearing relaxed and comfortable

Imagine that someone smiles at you, maintains comfortable eye contact with you, and speaks in gentle tones while saying, "I simply cannot stand to be with you." Perhaps it is easier to imagine someone glaring at you, decidedly placing his or her hands on the hips, and saying in a loud voice, "No. I am not mad at you." When words and nonverbal communications are inconsistent, people typically trust the nonverbal messages.

Be aware that personal space also differs by culture and developmental level. Some children are sensitive to sitting too close or being touched (e.g., a pat on the back). Asking permission or checking with students as well as adults first is respectful and prudent.

Nonverbal actions can be difficult to interpret and communicate because of cultural differences. For example, adults who were raised in Western cultures are usually quite comfortable with eye contact. A comfortable gaze is associated with presence and attention. However, in some, cultures eye contact is associated with disrespect. Thus, sensitivity to preferences and familiarity, typically communicated nonverbally, is essential.

Attention to our own nonverbal factors can also teach us more about ourselves. For example, Mary was in a consultation session with a parent. Her arms were crossed, and she appeared rigid—though she had a gentle smile on her face and her responses were accurate. When we watched the tape of the session, Mary realized that she was uncomfortable with the parent. She felt intimidated. Her crossed arms may have been an unconscious effort to protect herself.

TRACKING

Young children often communicate with actions or through play (as discussed in *Counseling Children and Adolescents in Schools*). School-based professionals acknowledge and respond to actions by tracking, which is a verbal response that identifies or describes a child's behavior. Additionally, they demonstrate their attention with tracking responses. For example, a counselor might say, "You are looking around the room to see what is here" or "You're trying to roll your sleeve." We also use a form of tracking with adolescents or adults by nodding our heads to show we are following the content, changing our facial expression to match the feeling or content of the message, and using minimal encouragers, such as *yes* or *okay*. Through the use of nonverbal attending and tracking, you establish that you are present and focused on the student client.

> Tour Guide Note: On this tour you will meet a few school counselors and school psychologists in addition to several student clients. For example, you will meet **Anita**, who is a seventh grade student. She is having one of those days when everything seems to go wrong, and people repeatedly misunderstand her. **Paul** is a senior who has encountered competing expectations from a variety of important people in his life. **Jeremy** is an athletic second grade boy who views himself as a team leader. **Teriqua** is a sophomore who is originally from Ethiopia. Adjusting to her new school has been fairly easy; making new friends has been incredibly difficult. Later, you will become acquainted with **Juan**, a high achieving junior who is tired and discouraged.

PARAPHRASING

We communicate our understanding of clients and their situations by paraphrasing (sometimes called reflecting content). In other words, we use a combination of student clients' words and our own to "reflect back" what we have heard. In our first example, the school psychologist paraphrases Anita's difficult day.

Anita, a seventh grade student: It was a terrible day. First of all Bill asked me to help him with his creative writing assignment. Beth became angry at both of us because she wanted him to go skating with her. And then Dad got mad at me because I got home late.

School Psychologist: Your day has been tough because you were trying to help Bill, and people got mad at you.

In this second example, the school counselor paraphrases Paul's many responsibilities.

Paul, a senior: I'm not sure where to start. I have to get applications for college and financial aid ready. I have a major assignment due in chem. My mom needs me to help get the house ready for company, and Beth wants to go to the movies.

School Counselor: You have so many things you need to do. Applications are due. Assignments are due. You have responsibilities at home. And Beth wants you to spend time with her.

Because paraphrasing is fairly straightforward, the responses may seem like mimicking or parroting. The challenge is to succinctly capture the essence of the content as well as the aspects of the content that are most important. Additionally, we listen for core messages, themes, and perceptions. Our goal is to understand the other person as fully and accurately as possible.

REFLECTING AFFECT

Our responses become stronger when we reflect *affect* (or feelings) as well as content. Reflecting affect adds the dimension of inferring another person's feelings regarding the content. In the following example, the school counselor (SC) reflects both aspects of Jeremy's statement.

Jeremy: It isn't fair. I was supposed to be captain of the soccer team, and then when Jill came, everyone did what she said to do.

SC: You're *angry* because you thought you would be the captain.

In this longer exchange with Teriqua, notice how the school counselor continues to reflect content and affect.

Teriqua: I came to this school two months ago. I know my way around and I'm doing okay in my classes. But I still haven't made any friends.

SC: Even though you feel fairly comfortable with the building and schedule, you are *lonely* and want to be included.

Teriqua: Yeah. I didn't have trouble making new friends in Ethiopia. And I had lots of them. What's going on here?

SC: You're *confused* because finding new friends was easy for you in Ethiopia.

Teriqua: Yeah. I was in lots of clubs. I played soccer. I knew everyone.

SC: And now you go to classes and try to figure out what's not working for you here.

Teriqua: Sometimes I think kids here are just not friendly. And then sometimes I think it's because I'm different.

SC: I'm guessing that you're *worried* that your difficulty is related to your being from another country.

With practice, professional helpers reflect affect with short phrases, such as "You are angry" or "This has been scary for you." Notice how the same goal of helping Teriqua tell her story can be met with shortened reflections.

Teriqua: I came to this school two months ago. I know my way around and I'm doing okay in my classes. But I still haven't made any friends.

SC: You are *lonely* and want to be included.

Teriqua: Yeah. I didn't have trouble making new friends in Ethiopia. And I had lots of them. What's going on here?

SC: This is *confusing* for you.

Teriqua: Yeah. I was in lots of clubs. I played soccer. I knew everyone.

SC: You were accepted and you felt *secure*.

Teriqua: Sometimes I think kids here are just not friendly. And then sometimes I think it's because I'm different.

SC: You are *worried* that this has something to do with your being from another country.

An even more abbreviated form of a reflection is sometimes termed an *accent*. Accents highlight just one or two words from the student client's statement. For example, in Teriqua's last sentence she stated, "And then sometimes I think it's because I'm different." The school counselor could say, "Different?" as a way of inviting Teriqua to tell more about what different means to her.

Practicing Nonverbal Attending, Reflecting Content, and Reflecting Affect

1. Work in dyads, with Partner A and Partner B.

2. During the first 5 minutes, Partner A's role is to talk about a recent event that was somewhat perplexing or confusing. Partner B's role is to nonverbally communicate presence and attention, reflect content, and reflect affect.

3. After 5 minutes, Partner B can give feedback to Partner A. For example, the partner says, "Even though you weren't accurate in your reflection about my being irritated, I still knew you wanted to understand me because you tried to reflect. You sat calmly, and your arms and legs were uncrossed. You didn't seem to be in a hurry to do anything but listen. I liked that. You seemed to have trouble making eye contact with me."

4. During the next 5 minutes, Partner B's role is to talk about a pending decision while Partner A nonverbally communicates presence and attention, reflects content, and reflects affect.

5. Finally, Partner A should give feedback to Partner B.

How did you experience the experiment?

_____

_____

_____

_____

_____

What did you learn from it?

_____

_____

_____

_____

_____

Preservice professionals often struggle with reflecting affect. They find that they use the same words over and over. They have trouble with intensity. For example, they might say, "You seem a little sad about something" to someone who is crying. *Frustrated* and *upset* become default terms for reflecting affect.

Thus, we encourage preservice professional helpers to explore resources for developing their affective vocabulary. An electronic search using "feeling word list" and "feeling word chart" yields several useful resources. We also suggest participation in the following activity.

Developing Your Affective Vocabulary

1. In the first column, list all the synonyms you can for *happy*. Think about using feeling words reflective of different levels of intensity and different developmental levels.

_____	_____	Young Children
_____	_____	_____
_____	_____	_____

_____ _____ _____

_____ _____ Pre-adolescents

_____ _____ _____

_____ _____ _____

_____ _____ _____

_____ _____ Adolescents

_____ _____ _____

_____ _____ _____

_____ _____ _____

2. Use a thesaurus to increase your list to at least 10 synonyms for *happy*.

3. In the second column, rank the terms in order of intensity.

4. In the third column, list terms you would use for young children, pre-adolescents, and adolescents.

5. Repeat this exercise with *mad*, *sad*, and *afraid*.

CLARIFYING

Clarification responses are appropriate when professionals are uncertain about something that a student or an adult has said. Clarification responses also help others achieve personal clarity. Clarification statements can take the form of a question or a restatement with an explicit clarifying component (e.g., "Now, let me see if I have this straight").

> Tour Guide Note: In the following section you will be introduced to **Ben's parent**. The parent is quite frustrated because Ben has a history of behavior problems at school. Notice how the school psychologist (SP) uses clarification to ascertain an accurate understanding of this parent.

Parent: I'm so angry because Ben is in trouble again. It seems like all I do is come to school to deal with problems he gets himself into.

SP: It sounds like you are angry at Ben, and also frustrated because your many trips to school have not changed anything.

Parent: Yeah. I try so hard to be understanding because I know Ben's limitations are contributing to his behavioral problems, and sometimes I just run out of patience.

SP: I'm sorry. I'm not sure what limitations you are talking about. I only knew about some health related issues.

Parent: Yes, Ben has asthma, and his allergies sometimes interfere with his concentration.

SP: And you are seeing connections between the difficulties Ben has at school and his asthma.

Parent: Ben often has asthma attacks at night. Of course we're up several hours as we use his inhalers to help get his breathing regulated. During allergy season this happens more often. We're usually able to get things stabilized, but Ben loses so much energy in the process, and he doesn't get enough rest. He has trouble concentrating at school, and seems to be more irritable.

SP: Okay. Now I understand.

SUMMARIZING

Summarizing responses assist professional helpers particularly when starting a session, introducing a transition, or ending a session. With summaries, professionals capture the essence and key elements of a session or segment of a session. They provide additional evidence that the professional does, indeed, understand the messages the student has endeavored to communicate.

For example, in response to Teriqua's series of comments, a professional might say, "Even though you have been at this school for two months, you haven't been able to make many friends. This is a new experience for you because you had lots of friends in Ethiopia, and you were involved in many activities. You're confused and discouraged because you don't know what is going on for sure, and you don't know how to make more friends."

After a summary, a professional can facilitate a transition to problem solving or continue listening to assist the other person as the situation is explored. For example, a professional might introduce a transition in the session by saying, "Before we talk about how you can figure this confusing situation out, I'd like to be sure I fully understand what is going on for you. You want to be on the fourth grade soccer team, and you also want to be in the winter concert. Your friends want you to join their Odyssey of the Mind team. Your parents have said you can only participate in two of those activities, and you just don't know how to decide what to do."

> You may need to provide more summaries throughout the session for younger children. Frequent use of summaries is also helpful for student clients who move from topic to topic.

SKILLFUL USE OF QUESTIONS

Professional orientation to questions has changed over the years. Many of us who were trained several years ago were not allowed to ask any questions. I (S.M.) have a friend who failed an entire assignment because he asked one question on a taped counseling session. Our position is not quite so strong. Still, our preservice professionals complain because they cannot imagine how they can work without asking multiple questions.

We propose two categories of questions to aid professionals in working with students. *Information acquisition questions,* the first type, are clear requests for information (e.g., "Who is your advisor?"). Indeed, there are times when professionals need clear information to be responsibly helpful. However, as their facilitation skills develop, professional helpers learn that students often share the important information and tell their life stories on their terms when we track, reflect, and summarize.

Facilitative inquiries, the second type of questions, are designed to increase self-awareness, introspection, reflection, and exploration of optional meanings. Facilitative inquiries also assist student clients in clarifying goals, making plans to achieve goals, circumventing setbacks, and generalizing their success to other areas.

Well composed questions *are* therapeutic. However, it is important to remember that we are not interrogating attorneys! Additionally, we don't ask questions simply to fill the time or to satisfy our curiosity. Rather, questions are targeted at increasing self-understanding, insight, and resolution to challenges. Notice ways you can pose questions with versatility and for a variety of purposes:

- How was that for you? (invites reactions including thoughts, feelings, and assigned meaning)
- I have a hunch I'd like to check out with you. (tentatively poses a hypothesis)
- What are your thoughts about these three options? (encourages a cognitive response)
- What possibilities have you considered? (implies that student has considered options and that he or she has options)
- What challenges will you encounter this week? (assists in identifying challenges and planning strategies for maintaining progress)
- What day will be the most difficult for you? (implies the normalcy of difficult days and provides opportunity to circumvent difficulties that may arise)
- I'm wondering if you would be willing to talk about your reactions to Mr. Nillson. (empowers the student client to determine if he or she will answer and prevents a closed question trap)
- How will you know when you are ready to make the decision? (invites tangible indicators of progress toward goals)
- I'm wondering what you said to yourself about missing the deadline. (introduces a cognitive focus that may be useful for intervention)
- I'm wondering how it would be for you to try out for the play, knowing you may not get the part. (assists student in achieving self-understanding and potentially increased courage)
- Who will be the first to notice that you have taken responsibility for training rules? (identifies indicators of success as well as potentially supportive individuals)
- To whom will you turn for support when you feel discouraged or tempted to violate training rules? (assists student in identifying sources of encouragement and circumventing potential setbacks)

It is important to consider the cognitive development of students when posing questions. Younger children and some adolescents are not able to understand or respond to an inquiry requiring abstract thought.

Generating Questions

Asking questions that truly encourage deeper reflection and exploration is more difficult than it seems. As a practice exercise, generate as many questions as you can in response to Juan, who is a junior in high school: "What's the use? I am tired of school. I am tired of working this hard. Why should I beat my head against the wall so I can go to college, just so I can go on to med school? I would just as soon get my G.E.D. and get a job doing something. If I go to med school it will be years before I can start earning a decent living."

_____

_____

_____

_____

_____

_____

_____

One of the many challenges when acquiring information is to refrain from asking questions to satisfy our own curiosity. Good questions to frequently ask yourself are "What do I need to know in order to be responsibly helpful?" and "Do I need to know the answer to this question?" Another self-monitoring strategy is to ask, "What is my purpose in asking this question?" To assist our trainees in making these decisions, we have used the model prepared by Sklare, Portes, and Splete (1985) for assessing the efficacy of questions used in counseling sessions. Questions are given an effectiveness score from –4 to +4 as shown in Figure 2.1.

Irrelevant questions are rated as –4. They misdirect attention of the student and professional helper. These irrelevant questions evidence professional helpers' incompetence, inattentiveness, and possibly resistance. For Juan, a –4 question might be, "Who is your medical doctor?"

"Why" questions are prime examples of –3 questions, which often result in defensiveness. They sometimes stem from helpers' values and may be received as accusatory. They often become another barrier to communication. For Juan,

Figure 2.1 Questioning Effectiveness Model

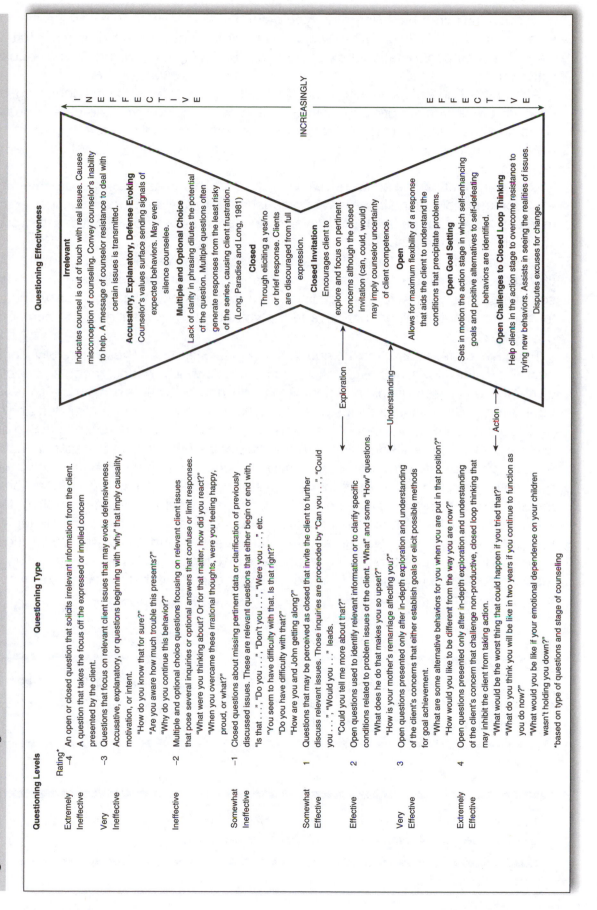

Questioning Levels | **Questioning Type** | **Questioning Effectiveness**

Rating*

Extremely Ineffective —4
An open or closed question that solicits irrelevant information from the client. A question that takes the focus off the expressed or implied concern presented by the client.

Irrelevant
Indicates counsel is out of touch with real issues. Causes misconception of counseling. Convey counselor's inability to help. A message of counselor resistance to deal with certain issues is transmitted.

Very Ineffective —3
Questions that focus on relevant client issues that may evoke defensiveness. Accusative, explanatory, or questions beginning with "why" that imply causality, motivation, or intent.

"How do you know that for sure?"
"Are you aware how much trouble this presents?"
"Why do you continue this behavior?"

Accusatory, Explanatory, Defense Evoking
Counselor's values surface sending signals of expected behaviors. May even silence counselee.

Ineffective —2
Multiple and optional choice questions focusing on relevant client issues that pose several inquiries or optional answers that confuse or limit responses.

"What were you thinking about? Or for that matter, how did you react?"
"When you overcame these irrational thoughts, were you feeling happy, proud, or what?"

Multiple and Optional Choice
Lack of clarity in phrasing dilutes the potential of the question. Multiple questions often generate responses from the least risky of the series, causing client frustration.

Somewhat Ineffective —1
Closed questions about missing pertinent data or clarification of previously discussed issues. These are relevant questions that either begin or end with,

"Is that . . .", "Do you . . .", "Don't you . . .", "Were you . . .", etc.
"You seem to have difficulty with that. Is that right?"
"Do you have difficulty with that?"
"How are you and John getting along?"

Closed
Through eliciting a yes/no or brief response. Clients are discouraged from full expression.
(Long, Paradise and Long, 1981)

Somewhat Effective 1
Questions that may be perceived as closed that invite the client to further discuss relevant issues. Those inquiries are proceeded by "Can you . . .", "Could you . . .", "Would you . . ." leads.

"Could you tell me more about that?"

Closed Invitation
Encourages client to explore and focus on pertinent concerns although the closed invitation (can, could, would) may imply counselor uncertainty of client competence.

— Exploration →

Effective 2
Open questions used to identify relevant information or to clarify specific conditions related to problem issues of the client. "What" and some "How" questions.

"What does he do that makes you so upset?"
"How is your mother's remarriage affecting you?"

Open
Allows for maximum flexibility of a response that aids the client to understand the conditions that precipitate problems.

— Understanding →

Very Effective 3
Open questions presented only after in-depth exploration and understanding of the client's concerns that either establish goals or elicit possible methods for goal achievement.

"What are some alternative behaviors for you when you are put in that position?"
"How would you like to be different from the way you are now?"

Open Goal Setting
Sets in motion the action stage in which self-enhancing goals and positive alternatives to self-defeating behaviors are identified.

— Action →

Extremely Effective 4
Open questions presented only after in-depth exploration and understanding of the client's concern that challenge non-productive, closed loop thinking that may inhibit the client from taking action.

"What would be the worst thing that could happen if you tried that?"
"What do you think you will be like in two years if you continue to function as you do now?"
"What would you be like if your emotional dependence on your children wasn't holding you down?"

*based on type of questions and stage of counseling

INEFFECTIVE ← INCREASINGLY → EFFECTIVE

INCREASINGLY

27

a –3 question might be, "Where did you get the idea that you could make a decent salary with a G.E.D.?" or "Why would you want to throw such a promising future away?" A less confrontational example might be, "Why did you bring your books with you?"

Although –2 questions are not as destructive to relationships, they are confusing, or they narrow response options. Questions rated as –2 include multiple choice questions, such as, "Juan, would you rather go to a community college to get started, or would you rather go straight to the university?" Posing a series of questions is also rated as –2.

Questions that can be answered with a single word, such as *yes* or *no*, are rated as –1. Such questions stand in the way of broader self-exploration. Sometimes, they communicate covert advice, such as, "Have you thought about exploring options for working while you take classes?"

Questions rated as +1 are also closed. They are positive because they invite further discussion. The problem is that they can also be answered in one word, and sometimes that word is *no*. A +1 question for Juan might be, "Would you be willing to tell me some of the things that have led to you questioning your goal to become a physician?"

Effective professionals most frequently ask +2 questions. These carefully composed questions invite self-exploration; thus, they allow the broadest range and depth of responses. These questions often begin with *how* or *what*. An example of a +2 question is, "What kinds of things have led to you questioning your earlier decision?"

Questions rated as +3 and +4 are used less often. Their ratings relate to timing as well as phrasing. The +3 questions are asked after the professional *and* student have a thorough understanding of the presenting concern. They introduce or amplify the goal setting process. Questions in the +4 category often accompany +3 questions; these queries strengthen plans and propel energy for goal attainment. For Juan, the sequence might be, "When you encounter self-doubt again, what are some strategies you can use to protect yourself from discouragement?" and "What self-doubt messages will likely come up during your math test tomorrow?" The student client's response could be followed by "And how will you respond to that message so it won't keep pestering you?"

> Tour Guide Note: The last three questions are influenced by cognitive-behavioral approaches. Externalizing the problem, a narrative therapy intervention, is also helpful when student clients encounter self-doubt and negative self-talk.

Heed one word of caution: It is important to remember that when asked prematurely, +3 and +4 questions become –4 questions because they are irrelevant.

Return to the questions you wrote in response to Juan, and rank each one according to the model. Consider modifications you could make to your –2, –1, and +1 questions, so they would be +2 questions.

The form and the frequency of questions seem to present the greatest challenges for preservice and inservice professionals. Sometimes, they get stuck in question traps from which they can't find an escape. One question seems to beget another, and they quickly run out of ideas for what to ask next. Unfortunately, this type of exchange is not productive, and student clients become frustrated or dependent. If this type of interaction continues, the relationship may be damaged.

> One strategy for escaping a question trap is to say something like, "That wasn't how I wanted to phrase that. Let me try again."

Tour Guide Note: Using the same vignette from above, the following example illustrates an ineffective and unhelpful exchange between the school counselor (SC) and Juan. It may also provide comic relief ☺.

Juan: What's the use? I am tired of school. I am tired of working this hard. Why should I beat my head against the wall so I can go to college, just so I can go on to med school? I would just as soon get my G.E.D. and get a job doing something. If I go to med school it will be years before I can start earning a decent living.

SC: Where do you want to go?

Juan: Well, I would like to get started in the university here in town; the community college is a possibility. I've also thought about going to a private college in Kansas.

SC: Is that the college in Hastings?

Juan: Yes.

SC: Did you get all the applications?

Juan: No.

SC: Why?

Juan: I don't know, I wasn't sure how to start.

SC: How about financial aid? Can your folks get that information in on time so you'll be eligible?

Juan: If I could get them some information on how to do that, I'm sure they can.

SC: Why are you thinking about going to the community college?

Juan: I'm really not. I wanted to learn about my options, and how much everything will cost. I also thought I should apply to more than one place.

SC: Why? Do you think you won't get accepted?

Juan: I really don't know.

> Tour Guide Note: The school counselor (SC) in the following example combines reflection and questions to help Juan explore his frustration and discouragement. With this type of interaction, the SC is able to obtain a clearer understanding of Juan's difficulties.

Juan: What's the use? I am tired of school. I am tired of working this hard. Why should I beat my head against the wall so I can go to college, just so I can go on to med school? I would just as soon get my G.E.D. and get a job doing something. If I go to med school it will be years before I can start earning a decent living.

SC: You're exhausted from studying so hard, and then when you consider how many years you will have to work this hard to be an M.D., you become discouraged and overwhelmed.

Juan: It doesn't even take that long to get discouraged. All I have to do is walk into the calculus room and think about all the assignments that I have due. When that happens I just want to walk out the door and quit.

SC: Calculus just seems like this incredible barrier right now. What has happened in calculus that has become so difficult for you?

Juan: Well, I think I had a fairly good handle on it last semester. I did okay in January too, and then I got sick and missed a whole week of school. I missed out on several things, and nothing has made sense since then.

SC: You felt fairly comfortable with calculus all through the first semester, but getting sick in January really set you back.

Juan: I got behind in everything else then too. When I came back to school I really didn't feel good. I was behind in everything, and then didn't have the energy I usually have. Things went south pretty fast.

SC: And how is your health now?

Juan: I am starting to feel pretty good again. I haven't started working out like I used to, but hope to get back on track with that during spring break. I had mono, and didn't really believe the physicians when they said it would take a long time to get my strength back. I have never missed much school, and whenever I've been sick, it's just been for a few days.

SC: You were awfully sick, and you're still surprised that it has taken so long to really feel good again—even though the physicians told you it would take a long time.

Juan: That's for sure. And it has really messed me up. My grades have dropped in several classes.

SC: It sounds like doing well in school is important to you.

Juan: Well, it always has been. I really want to go to college and I think I want to go to med school. My parents don't have that kind of money so I'm going to have to get some scholarships. If I don't get my grades back up, I won't be able to do that.

SC: So, as you see it now, a low grade in calculus would become a barrier to getting scholarships so you can go to college.

Juan: It's more than that. I want to go to the U, and their admission requirements are really high. Tuition at the U is high too. I really need to figure out a way to pull out of this.

SC: Doing well in school is important to you for several reasons. You want to be a physician, and to prepare for med school you want to go to the University of Alabama. Your grades have been good, so you are in line for a scholarship. You're discouraged because you've never been as sick as you were this semester, and that really set you back in calculus. Even though you're discouraged and worried about your grades, you're still holding onto your dream.

Juan: That sums the mess up. Is there anything I can do to turn this around?

SC: What are some of the things you have tried?

> Tour Guide Note: Notice that the SC let Juan dictate when they would move from the situation to an implied goal. That segue suggests that the SC thought Juan was ready to begin the problem solving process.

As mentioned at the beginning of this section, some questions are asked to acquire important information. Professional helpers are skillful in discerning information they need to be helpful. They overcome their own curiosity, and they ask questions judiciously to avoid an interrogative interaction. They also recognize when using a question to facilitate clarification is appropriate. If too many questions are used, students tend to offer less information and wait for the helper's next question. This pattern is especially true of younger children who are used to responding to adults' requests.

PITFALLS TO AVOID

We have reviewed basic skills of counseling that are particularly helpful when endeavoring to develop solid working relationships with individuals of all ages. In this section, we call attention to communication roadblocks based on an original list of barriers identified by Thomas Gordon (1970, 1974). Even though Gordon's list of barriers was originally published over 40 years ago, contemporary authors continue to build on his work as we have.

> We learn some strategies.
> We unlearn or avoid others!

Table 2.1   Communication Roadblocks (adapted from Gordon's twelve roadblocks to communication, Gordon, 1970, 1974)

Roadblock	Examples
Bossing	• Go back to your classroom and tell your teacher what you have done. • Get out of that line immediately and finish your spelling.
Threatening	• I will take away your recess for the rest of the year if we have one more disruption.
Preaching and lecturing	• You are much too nice of a child to act like that. Your parents would be so disappointed if I told them about this. • If I've told you once, I've told you 100 times that you must start thinking about your future right now.
Giving advice	• If I were you, I would just talk with the other girls in your class and tell them how you feel. • You just need to ignore that boy and get on with your life. • You should just lower your expectations and go to the community college here in town.
Criticizing and judging	• You are so lazy! How could you possibly get a good grade when you didn't even try? • Your appearance is disrespectful and disgusting. You should be ashamed of yourself. I am.
Interrogating	• Why did you do it this way? • Where did you leave your homework and backpack?
Distracting or changing the subject	• Say, have you heard about that new movie downtown? • Let's play a game, so you can forget about your worries.
Making sarcastic comments	• How did you think it would turn out?! • That was stupid. • You run like a girl!
Mind reading	• I know. You are mad at me because I came in late. • You think I'm supposed to help you all the time because I'm smarter.
Psychologizing	• I know what your problem is. You are still having problems adjusting to your new home. • You are so defensive.
One upping	• You think you have problems. Mine are much worse than yours.
Minimizing and placating	• In 3 years, you will have forgotten all about this. • You're stewing and fretting over something as ridiculous as that? • You'll be okay in just a few days. You are such a strong person that you will be able to get over this easily.
Assigning motives	• You hid from me on the playground because you did not want to be seen talking to me. • You did that to get even with me. • You are just trying to irritate me!

Although we typically avoid focusing on mistakes our preservice school counselors and school psychologists have made, we have found that it is helpful to identify common errors that we have observed and, for the record, errors that we made when we were graduate students! The following paragraphs include examples of pitfalls to avoid.

> These pitfalls are not unique to the counseling relationship. They interfere with all personal as well as professional communication.

How Do You Feel About That?

This common mistake may have originated in pop psychology and television sitcoms. Although professionals often focus on feelings with their reflections, asking students to identify their feelings rarely has value. The response is often cognition, and it seldom leads to productive work. Instead, we demonstrate our keen attention and understanding by reflecting *our* understanding of the student client's thoughts and feelings. If you are really unsure of what the feeling is behind a student's statement, try a general exploratory statement to help you understand the student's situation better—for example, "Boy! It sounds like you have so many different feelings going on inside of you right now. Help me understand what it's like for you to have your dad in jail."

Turning Good Reflections Into Questions

It is quite common for preservice professionals to communicate good reflections; however, they are unsure of themselves. Thus, they say something like, "You are angry at him, aren't you?" or "You are worried about your grades. Am I right?" Although these are not fatal errors, they may result in a one word response and interrupt the dialogue.

Focusing on a Third Party

Sometimes, it is important to inquire about our students' understanding of others' perceptions. Usually, however, focusing on someone external to the counseling relationship is less productive. Sometimes, adolescents attempt to deflect attention from themselves by focusing on friends and parents rather than on their own experiences and feelings. Examples of focusing on a third party include such questions as, "How does your father feel about you going to the university?" or "What was he trying to accomplish?" Sometimes, helpers and student clients inadvertently collude in focusing on others because the work is less intense when the focus is on someone outside the counseling room.

Interchanging Think and Feel

Although *think* and *feel* are not synonyms, they are often substituted for one another during informal conversations and even formal writing. For example, a helper might say, "You feel that he was wrong when he accused you." The helper likely believes this response reflected feelings; actually, no feelings are involved in this statement.

We encourage you to develop a habit of using the terms accurately. Correct use of both terms helps you reflect more precisely and more poignantly. Additionally, you will be laying groundwork for when you endeavor to help student clients discern their thoughts from their feelings, particularly as you work from cognitive-behavioral and problem solving approaches.

A clue for identifying when reference is being made to a cognition rather than an emotion is the use of the word *that* (e.g., "you feel that she should not be the captain"). Correct phrasing would be, "You think he was wrong to choose her for captain." Correct use of these verbs averts professionals' confusion when reflecting, and it helps student clients clarify their experiences.

Understating or Overstating the Intensity

Reflecting student clients' experiences with accurate intensity is often challenging. For example, professional helpers might say, "You are feeling just a little irritated," when the student client is furious. At other times, the reflections are so tentative that their value is diminished, as illustrated with "I'm not sure about this, but it sounds like you may be feeling a little bit anxious because of the test you have scheduled." These statements reduce the effectiveness of professionals' input. An inadvertent implication might be that the helper doesn't think the presenting problem is important.

Vaguely Focused Reflections

Preservice professionals often have trouble using precise and personalized language. For example, people often say, "How's it going today?" Of course, they mean, "How are you today?" or "How's your day been?" Sometimes, professionals say, "There's some anger there." Of course, anger is not freely floating in the atmosphere somewhere; the student is experiencing anger. As you reflect, strive for crisp, targeted language.

> Consider use of formal versus informal language. Informality can reduce your effectiveness. On the other hand, informality is more engaging for some students.

Advice Couched as a Question

Preservice professionals sometimes have difficulty letting go of the notion that much of our work is giving advice or telling children, youth, parents, or teachers what to do. That approach rarely works. If it were effective, children would be champions in multiple arenas because they get so much advice from so many sources.

Covert advice is not effective either, and it's dishonest. For example, "Have you asked him to help you with the problem?" probably means, "I think you should ask him to help you with the problem." Similarly, "Why don't you stand up to your friends?" is not a good question, and it may not be good advice.

Asking Closed Questions and Creating Question Traps

Particularly with children and youth, closed questions yield minimal answers. Without an adequate response, professionals typically ask another closed question and find themselves in a question trap. Open-ended questions are more beneficial than closed questions; however, they can also result in a question trap if too many are asked or they are not properly balanced with reflections.

BEFORE YOU CONDUCT YOUR FIRST SESSION OR A SESSION IN AN UNFAMILIAR SITUATION

Undoubtedly, you will be nervous before you see your first student client for individual counseling or when you facilitate your first counseling group. We are sometimes anxious and question our abilities when we initiate a counseling relationship, and we've done this work for many years! Even Carl Whitaker, a well-known family therapist, often said he was anxious before seeing clients, particularly for the first time. In other words, a certain level of anxiety is normal.

It may be helpful to remind yourself of the most important task of the first session: facilitating a relationship. The person with whom you are working will probably not notice if your responses are awkward and if you ask closed questions. That individual will likely be anxious as well and may be afraid of being judged or criticized. During the first few minutes, we lay the foundation for how the relationship will develop. Thus, it is important to communicate acceptance, respect, warmth, and your understanding of his or her experience. It is also important to help persons in distress regain a sense of hope.

Typically, professional development proceeds from reading and hearing about counseling skills, practicing in groups, and practicing in role plays to conducting an actual session under supervision. Anxiety, self-doubt, and self-consciousness are common during early sessions. This kind of anxiety, as described by two of our preservice school counselors at the end of their first practicum, is actually normal.

Testimonial of Sheila Phelps: I went into practicum with very little anxiety. I thought I knew what to expect and felt confident that I would make it through. That all changed after the first week. Even though I had been involved in several role plays in other classes, read the book, and had my list of feeling words memorized, the thought that this was no longer a role play, but a real experience with a real client had me tied up in knots. The first time I sat across from my client felt like an eternity. I questioned my abilities and felt myself being overly critical with how I presented myself to my client. Actually, finishing out my professional career as a classroom science teacher didn't look that bad after all. I asked myself on several occasions at the beginning of the practicum journey, "What do you think you are doing? Who do you think you are? What do you know about counseling?"

It took a couple of weeks to work through my apprehension, self-doubts, and internal struggle of whether or not I would be effective as a counselor. Through the gentle guidance of my supervisor, and the support of the other five members of our practicum team, I realized that I was not alone in this. I had six other people behind the mirror cheering me on, offering valuable feedback, and helping me develop both professionally and personally. Observing my other team members and learning from their experience as well as my own was tremendous. Toward the end of practicum I was able to start formulating answers to those self-doubt questions I had at the beginning. My feelings of apprehension and self-doubts melted as I gained confidence in my abilities as a counselor.

Practicum is a process and a journey. I could not imagine a richer experience.

Testimonial of Sherri Schmidke: Practicum was one of the greatest and maybe the greatest experiences I have had in this program (and that says a lot). Going in to prac I was extremely nervous about how I was going to say the wrong thing and mess someone up, or that the clients would see me as an inexperienced student that didn't have the slightest clue of what I was doing. The mirror was the greatest cause of my anxiety, mostly because it was an unknown.

In eight weeks I gained confidence and an enjoyment for counseling far beyond my wildest dreams. My supervisor told me she didn't know who changed more: the client or myself. Practicum is a growth experience without the growing pains. I enjoyed every minute of it, and I was sad to see the end come. (Which was huge for me because I didn't even want to do practicum because of the time commitment!) After my first session with my first client I was pumped. I looked forward to my session every week. I don't know where I learned more, watching my peers counsel or being in the room myself. Both were truly learning experiences in very different ways. I will never forget my time in practicum, and I am very grateful for the experience it was—both for my future career and for myself personally.

USING SKILLS IN COMBINATION

Nonverbally attending, tracking, paraphrasing, reflecting, clarifying, summarizing, and skillfully asking questions are not isolated skills. As professionals learn to use all of these techniques, the art of our work becomes more obvious. Rarely, though, does that artistry appear without practice. Thus, we encourage you to practice during conversations with friends and while observing other people. For example, practice reflecting while you watch television. You might say, "She looks angry" or "He is happy because the girl said she would help him with the homework." You might reflect as you go through checkout lines in stores, but be careful! You may start a conversation that will take longer than you expected! Remember that becoming a skillful school-based professional takes time.

Reflection Rx:

For each of these reflections, indicate what is problematic and compose an improved response.

You feel that your mom was being incredibly unfair.

Problem: _____

_____

Improvement: _____

_____

I'm wondering what your mom was feeling when your brother stormed out of the room.

Problem: _____

_____

Improvement: _____

_____

You're feeling sad and confused that you weren't invited to the party. Is that right?

Problem: _____

_____

Improvement: _____

_____

You're maybe feeling a little hurt that your boyfriend invited someone else to the dance.

Problem: _____

_____

Improvement: _____

_____

Boy, there's just a lotta feelings goin' on there.

Problem: _____

_____

Improvement: _____

_____

Question Rx

For each of these questions, indicate what is problematic and compose an improved one.

Why did you leave your homework at Don's house?

Problem: _____

_____

Improvement: _____

_____

How do you feel about what she said to you?

Problem: _____

_____

Improvement: _____

_____

Were you hoping to get even, or were you trying to explain your situation?

Problem: _____

_____

Improvement: _____

_____

You're angry about that, aren't you?

Problem: _____

_____

Improvement: _____

_____

Have you thought about talking with your parents about how you feel?

Problem: _____

_____

Improvement: _____

_____

Think and Feel Rx

For each of the following, indicate whether or not the words *think* and *feel* are used correctly.

1. I feel like shouting when I get out of class on Friday.
2. I feel that no one really understands my problems.
3. I am thinking about going to the dentist right now, and I feel scared about it.
4. I feel terrified whenever I am around snakes.
5. I feel like I'm 10 feet tall when someone tells me I'm smart.
6. I feel really angry because I trusted my friend, and she told someone what I had asked her to keep secret.
7. I feel like I haven't got a friend in the world.
8. I just crashed my car, and I feel that wasn't fair. After all, I just got it paid for last month.
9. I feel happy about buying some new clothes on Saturday. At the same time, I feel worried about my folks' reaction when they get the bill.
10. I feel so misunderstood.

Reflecting Content and Affect

Write a reflection of both content and affect for each of these comments:

Isabella, a fourth grade student: I couldn't go to baseball practice because I had to finish my math assignment, and then, I had to watch my baby sister while Dad ran some errands. Now, the coach won't let me play on the team this weekend. I guess it doesn't matter that much really.

Reflection:

_____

_____

_____

English teacher: I don't know what else I can do. The kids haven't learned their basic equations and the state tests are next week. I don't know what will happen if my kids don't meet bench marks.

Reflection:

_____

_____

_____

Parent of seventh grade girl: I'm so angry at the girls in Annie's class. They are so mean to her. They call her names. They leave her out of their activities. They make fun of her clothes. They are absolutely cruel!

Reflection:

_____

_____

_____

Tenth grade boy: I just found out I didn't make the cheerleading squad. I knew I could do the stunts if I had time, and I really wanted to be a varsity cheerleader. I didn't even care when other guys made fun of me. I wanted to be on the squad.

Reflection:

_____

_____

_____

Senior: What's the use? No matter how hard I try, I'll never get my SAT scores high enough to get a scholarship, and I know my parents won't pay for college. I may as well go out and find a job.

Reflection:

_____

_____

_____

Composing Facilitative Inquiry: +2 Questions

Compose two +2 facilitative inquiries that would improve each of the following questions:

Professional helper: Why did you ask me to see you today?

Inquiry 1:

_____

_____

_____

Inquiry 2:

_____

_____

_____

Professional helper: Can I help you?

Inquiry 1:

_____

_____

_____

Inquiry 2:

_____

_____

_____

Professional helper: Will you promise me that you'll come to school tomorrow?

Inquiry 1:

_____

_____

_____

Inquiry 2:

_____

_____

_____

Professional helper: Where do you want to go to college?

Inquiry 1:

_____

_____

_____

Inquiry 2:

_____

_____

_____

Professional helper: What do you want to do after you graduate from our school?

Inquiry 1:

_____

_____

_____

Inquiry 2:

_____

_____

_____

Professional helper: How bad are your grades?

Inquiry 1:

_____

_____

_____

Inquiry 2:

_____

_____

_____

Professional helper: What did you do in the lunch room before the monitor sent you to see me?

Inquiry 1:

_____

_____

_____

Inquiry 2:

_____

_____

_____

Professional helper: What were you and your friends doing on the playground before you began to cry?

Inquiry 1:

_____

_____

_____

Inquiry 2:

_____

_____

_____

Composing Facilitative Inquiry: +3 Questions

Questions become +3 when they are well timed and when they engage student clients in the process of setting goals. Assume you are working with Cassie (the student client featured in _Counseling Children and Adolescents in Schools_) and that you are confident she is ready to establish direction for her work with you. Combine your style and your knowledge of effective questions to compose three questions you might ask:

Inquiry 1:

_____

_____

_____

Inquiry 2:

_____

_____

_____

Inquiry 3:

_____

_____

_____

Composing Facilitative Inquiry: +4 Questions

Questions qualify for +4 when they build on the previous work and support goal attainment. These queries help students identify and prepare for roadblocks, possible setbacks, and challenges that might develop. Again, working with Cassie, compose two +4 questions to follow her responses to your +3 questions previously identified.

Inquiry 1:

_____

_____

_____

Inquiry 2:

_____

_____

_____

Composition of Advanced Facilitative Inquiry

In response to Cassie's comments that follow, compose at least two facilitative inquiries that you believe would be helpful, and one question that would *not* be helpful.

Cassie: I don't know. I'm struggling with so many questions about myself right now. Maybe there's something wrong with me. Worse yet, maybe I'm a bad kid.

Inquiry 1:

_____

_____

_____

Inquiry 2:

_____

_____

_____

Inappropriate/Nonfacilitative question:

_____

_____

_____

Cassie: What's the use? Even if I go to college, I probably won't get a job. I know lots of our school's alums who graduated from college, and they're still waiting tables. They can make more money waiting tables than they could if they used their degree.

Inquiry 1:

_____

_____

_____

Inquiry 2:

_____

_____

_____

Inappropriate/Nonfacilitative question:

_____

_____

_____

Cassie: What would you do if you were me? Have you ever wondered if you were queer?

> Question from the Tour Guides: Does a question seem appropriate to you here? How would you combine a question with a solid reflection?

Inquiry 1:

_____

_____

_____

Inquiry 2:

_____

_____

_____

Inappropriate/Nonfacilitative question:

_____

_____

_____

Imagine that you are sitting with Cassie. What is going on with you right now? What reactions and words came to your mind?

> Questions from the Tour Guides: What thoughts and feelings might underlie the questions Cassie verbally expressed? Would it be more helpful to respond with a reflection, a question, or a reflection and a question?

Compose a response that you believe would be most helpful for Cassie.

_____

_____

_____

_____

Compose a second response that you believe would be helpful for Cassie.

_____

_____

_____

_____

1. Of all the skills presented in this tour, which are the hardest for you?

_____

_____

_____

_____

_____

2. What personal attributes will help you master basic helping skills?

_____

_____

_____

_____

3. What can you do to alleviate your anxiety when working with student clients?

_____

_____

_____

_____

_____

Resources That Might Be Helpful for the Journey:

Cowles, J. (1997). Lessons from "The Little Prince": Therapeutic relationships with children. *Professional School Counseling, 1,* 57–60.

> Tour Guide Note: Cowles captured the essence of our work with children in this delightful article.

Faber, A., & Mazlish, E. (1992). *How to talk so kids will listen and listen so kids will talk.* New York: Avon.

> Tour Guide Note: Although this text is nearly 20 years old, we still recommend it for school counselors, school psychologists, and parents.

Van Velsor, P. (2004). Revisiting basic counseling skills with children. *Journal of Counseling and Development, 82,* 313–318.

TOUR 3

Departure!

Advanced Facilitation Skills

Learning Objectives

- Understand the role of empathy in your work with children and adolescents
- Understand the differences between "insight" for children, adolescents, and adults
- Apply immediacy, self-disclosure, challenging, reflecting meaning, and interpretation to student clients' comments
- Explore and make sense of the notion of therapeutic "use of self"
- Recognize the importance of respect for cultural differences when using all counseling skills and strategies

Tour Guide Note: As an orientation to the third tour of your journey, we have provided a review of empathy and its importance in our work. As we introduce advanced skills, you will become acquainted with **Jerome**, who is a sophomore. Jerome is frustrated because his teachers, his girlfriend, and his coach are all "on his case." You will briefly meet **Spencer**, who is an African American high school student. A sixth grade student, **Jill**, is worried about her grades and what will happen if she does not pass. **Ruth** is a high school student who is ambivalent and troubled by her relationship with her parents. **Ricardo**, a boy in ninth grade, is struggling because of relationship problems with his girlfriend. **Jose** is a senior who is dealing with a psychological bully. **Chi-Chen** feels desperate and ashamed because his SAT results do not meet criteria for admission at the university of his choice. We'll conclude this tour with a discussion about professional helpers' personal qualities and how they allow us to demonstrate our authenticity, respect, and empathy to enhance engagement between themselves and the students with whom they work.

As we mentioned on the previous tours, our preparatory activities led to concepts and skills that you will use throughout your professional journey. Sequence, labels, and applications are arbitrary. As you become more experienced with building helping relationships, you will recognize when student clients are ready to explore issues at deeper levels or, conversely, when you need to return to relationship building. Pacing and determining which skill to use for which student at which time are aspects of the art of counseling. One of the underlying prerequisites to the appropriate use of these skills is that professionals are able to empathize with students. The following review of empathy is offered as an orientation for Tour 3.

EMPATHY: THEORY AND RESEARCH

Empathy is our ability to, first, accurately understand someone's thoughts and feelings and then to communicate our understanding in a way that helps the other person *feel* understood. Empathy is a vital aspect of our work; it represents our efforts to comprehend how students and adults perceive their world. As with some of the other skills, this may seem deceptively simplistic. As a counselor educator friend once noted, "Empathy. It's so basic. *And,* it's so advanced."

The work of Carl Rogers (1980) stands out as a resource for helping preservice professionals understand the process of empathy:

> An empathic way of being with another person has several facets. It means entering the private perceptual world of the other and becoming thoroughly at home in it. It involves being sensitive, moment by moment, to the changing felt meanings which flow in this other person, to the fear or rage or tenderness or confusion or whatever that he or she is experiencing. It means temporarily living in the other's life, moving about in it delicately without making judgments; it means sensing meanings of which he or she is scarcely aware, but not trying to uncover totally unconscious feelings, since this would be too threatening. (p. 142)

Empathy and its role in effecting change have been extensively examined by a variety of researchers (e.g., Greenberg, Watson, Elliott, & Bohart, 2001). Based on a comprehensive meta-analysis of 190 inquiries related to empathy and outcomes, Greenberg and his colleagues concluded that empathy is a primary factor in successful counseling and that success correlates with the extent to which clients feel understood by their therapists. They emphasized the comprehensive nature of empathy by saying,

> Going beyond the specific responses, the empathic therapist's primary task is to understand experiences rather than words. Truly empathic therapists do not parrot clients' words back or reflect only the content of words; instead, they understand overall goals as well as moment-to-moment experiences, both explicit and implicit. Empathy in part entails capturing the nuances and implications of what people say, and reflecting this back to them for their consideration. (p. 383)

Much of what has been written about empathy relates to adults; less is known about the role that empathy plays in relation to our work with children and adolescents.

However, your accurate understanding of students' worldviews will enable you to effectively use the advanced skills presented on this tour.

With immediacy, self-disclosure, challenging, reflecting meaning, and interpretation, school counselors and school psychologists help students develop insight (Hill, 2004). As they gain insight, students can think about situations or events from new perspectives, make connections, and understand why things happen as they do (Elliott et al., 1994).

Although some might argue that children do not develop insight in the same way that adults do, professional helpers can help even the youngest student understand alternative perspectives. As adolescents gain insight into their own behavior, and the behavior of others, they lay groundwork for taking responsibility for their behavior and moving toward positive change. As professionals hone advanced skills, they are able to reflect core messages and convey an understanding of a student client's total experience. Although presented in isolation, these various skills complement one another, much as the various sections of an orchestra produce harmonies that no single member of the orchestra can do.

Undoubtedly, you have learned about empathy and empathic understanding in several of your classes. What does it mean to you? How do you explain it to others? How do you know when you are empathic?

IMMEDIACY

Immediacy may be one of the more confusing or abstract counseling skills. It is also quite powerful. Gladding (2006) defined immediacy as "the ability of the counselor to discuss with the client the quality of their relationship and current interactions; a response by a counselor to something that just took place in the counseling session" (p. 72). Sometimes immediacy is a comment on or conversation about the helping relationship. It might be introduced with an invitation such as, "We've worked together for 4 weeks now. I'm wondering if you would be willing to talk with me about how we are working together."

Other immediacy responses are specific to an event or time in a session—for example, "I have the sense that something just happened. A few minutes ago it seemed like we were talking about something important, and on the same wave length. Then all of a sudden, I felt disconnected from you." Concrete descriptors, such as noticing children's facial expressions or behaviors when they talk about a topic, can enhance the effectiveness of immediacy. For example, a school psychologist might say, "I notice that when I mention that it's time for recess, your face looks really sad. It seems like going outside with your class is not very fun for you, and you'd rather stay here."

> Tour Guide Note: In the following exchange, the school psychologist (SP) *meta-communicates* (communicates about communication) about Jerome's situation and Jerome's interaction with the SP.

Jerome: I don't know what to do. My girlfriend is mad at me. My mom is mad at me. My teachers are on my case. I don't even care about the team any more. Nothing matters.

SP: You are discouraged about so many things. Important people are angry with you, and football has always been a high priority for you.

Jerome: Chantelle says I'm moody all the time. She's tired of trying to cheer me up. Mom says I'm a grump too. Mr. Speell got on me cuz I was sulking in class. I was just tired because we had a long practice.

SP: You're feeling discouraged and unhappy right now, and it sounds like you are tired of having people try to figure out what's going on.

Jerome: They're just being nosey. They want me to be happy all the time. Why don't they just let me just be who I am?

SP: Everyone is trying to get you to cheer up, and then Mrs. Anderson sent you to visit with me. I have an idea that sitting with yet another person who may try to get you to smile and be happy is the last thing you want to do.

Jerome: I don't care. It doesn't bother me none.

SP: Okay. But I have the sense that something is bothering you a lot.

Jerome: Aah. I'm okay. I can handle things that come along. I just wish people would get off my case.

SP: I'm going to have a hard time for awhile, because I'm afraid I may be getting on your case, and I won't even know it. I'm wondering what you would be willing to do so I'll know that I'm starting to irritate you too.

Jerome: Aah. You won't.

SP: Okay. Let's see what happens then. I'd like to go back to something you said earlier. I was a bit confused because I know how much you have loved football, and you mentioned that you didn't care about the team any more. And you haven't talked about that again. There's something in my gut that tells me that you're upset about something related to the team.

Jerome: It's no big deal to me. It's a big deal to everyone else.

SP: Hmm, your face looked so sad just now as you said that.

School counselors and school psychologists work with people who represent different age groups, different ethnic groups, different socioeconomic status groups, different religions, and so forth. Immediacy can help bridge those differences and mitigate misunderstanding. Comments in the context of cultural differences might include, "That is very important to you, and I want to understand what it means to you. Would you explain a bit more for me?" Another general statement of immediacy is, "I have the sense that I just said something that didn't land well."

Like other counseling skills and interventions, many factors should be considered when using immediacy. For example, professional helpers must consider the timing, the nature of the relationship, and their purpose. Immediacy can be powerful; at the same time, it can intimidate students and adults. Immediacy, like disclosure, can arise from professional helpers' desire and needs rather than from a desire to help. Immediacy and disclosure can also be used in conjunction with self-disclosure, which is discussed next.

Think about a situation in which you recently felt "unbalanced" or thought you were receiving mixed messages from someone. With that situation in mind, compose a statement that accurately reflects immediacy on your part without compromising respect or jeopardizing the relationship.

_____

_____

_____

_____

SELF-DISCLOSURE

Self-disclosure is "a *conscious*, intentional technique in which clinicians share information about their lives outside the counseling relationship" (Gladding, 2006, p. 128). Self-disclosures can help professionals communicate understanding of students because of a shared experience or feeling. As with other skills, there are different levels of use. Disclosures such as, "I also ate lunch in the cafeteria today," appear quite inconsequential. At the other extreme are highly personal, charged, and inappropriate disclosures such as, "When I was your age, I had sex with my boyfriend too." Many factors, such as timing and the degree to which rapport is established, affect the results of self-disclosure. Thus, it is important for professionals to use self-disclosure judiciously and in accordance with guidelines, which include the following:

- The content is age appropriate for the student.
- The disclosure is perceived by the student as relevant (Welch & Gonzalez, 1999).
- The intention is to promote the student client's self-understanding or change (Welch & Gonzalez, 1999).
- The disclosure is brief (Welch & Gonzalez, 1999).
- The disclosure is given to assist the student in some way, rather than to satisfy a need or desire of the professional.
- The disclosure is relatively infrequent. Erring with too infrequent use of this tool is better than too frequent.

For some children and adolescents, the idea that another person has experienced something similar to them comes as a surprise. A properly timed self-disclosure can help students feel understood; it can also deepen their relationship with the professional helper, help clarify their own thinking on the issue, and normalize their experiences.

During one session, I (R.S.H.) observed a preservice school psychologist talking with a 10-year-old boy about what it was like to have divorced parents and to have limited visitations with his father. The child seemed uncomfortable and tended to change the subject as the trainee attempted to explore this issue. The session changed dramatically when the trainee shared that he remembered what it was like when he saw his father only during the summers after his parents divorced. The student client became much more open, and the rapport with the trainee deepened.

Effective helpers use caution when disclosing to adolescents. Some adolescents believe that their experiences are unique; a helper's disclosure may result in students' feeling dismissed, or discounted. Self-disclosures based on incorrect assumptions of similarity can also be counterproductive.

Helpers must also use discernment in disclosure when student clients ask personal questions. It is quite common for children and parents to ask, "Do you have children?" or "How old are you?" Many of the guidelines previously listed apply, with the recommendation of returning the focus to the student client or parent as soon as possible. Pairing the response with a reflection can be useful, as illustrated in the following interaction between Ricardo and his school counselor, Ian:

Ricardo, a freshman:	Of course I'm mad. Did your girlfriend ever break up with you and go out with your best friend?
Ian:	You're hurt because your girlfriend broke up with you, and you're particularly angry because she and your friend betrayed you.
Ricardo:	Well—wouldn't you be mad too?
Ian:	I'd be mad, and hurt, and I think I'd probably feel a lot of other things too, like embarrassed or humiliated. How does that fit for you?

Notice how Ian responds to Ricardo's next question without additional disclosure in the following interaction:

Ricardo:	I just don't know what I should do. What do you think?
Ian:	You're feeling stuck, and wish someone would just give you an answer. You still hope that your girlfriend will change her mind, and you wish I could tell you some ways to get that to happen.

As you can see, Ricardo's questions were expressions of his own experience and desperation. Ian could have diverted the focus of the session to himself by disclosing his previous experiences or even his suggestions for Ricardo. In all likelihood, neither would have been helpful, and it would have been more difficult to refocus on Ricardo.

> Tour Guide Note: Notice how the school counselor (SC) uses immediacy and self-disclosure to address differences in the following dialogue with Spencer.

SC: Spencer, I've been thinking about something. We've known each other three years, since you came to the high school. We've talked off and on, for various reasons during the time we've known each other. We have talked about some of the ways we are alike, we haven't talked about some of the ways we are different. It's no secret that I am a woman, and I'm quite a bit older than you. I'm also Latina and you're African American. Sometimes I worry that I say things or do things that mean something different to you than I intended.

Spencer: What do you mean?

SC: Well, for example, a few minutes ago you mentioned your girlfriend, and that you were worried about going to college, and how that would affect your girlfriend. I smiled as you said that, and then we quickly talked about something else. I wonder if the way I smiled suggested to you that I didn't think your concern was important—like I was being a grandmother type and implying, "Don't worry about such a silly thing as that."

Spencer: I didn't think about it that way. I was embarrassed that I brought it up. Maybe I did think that wasn't important for you.

SC: Thanks for thinking about that, Spencer. I was moved by your caring comments about your girlfriend, and that's why I smiled.

When you think about self-disclosure in a counseling session, what topics arouse discomfort for you?

_____

_____

_____

When have you disclosed something in a relationship and later regretted it?

_____

_____

_____

Do you think you would be inclined to self-disclose too much or too little?

_____

_____

_____

Think about a somewhat conflictual (minor) experience you recently encountered with someone. With that situation in mind, compose a statement that accurately discloses your experience without compromising respect or jeopardizing the relationship.

_____

_____

_____

CHALLENGING

Challenging, sometimes referred to as confrontation, is a response designed to explicate discrepancies (inconsistencies or incongruence), and encourage a resolution. For example, you may become aware of inconsistency between words and facial expressions, purported values and behavior, stated goals or desires and behavior, or things students say and their behavior. Appropriate responses to these areas of incongruity include helper responses such as these:

- I heard you say that you are so happy and that everything is going well. Yet your face looks sad, and your eyes are red as if you have been crying.
- Your words were, "I am fine." Your fists are clenched and your voice is loud and firm. They seem to be saying, "I am angry."
- You mentioned that you are really uncomfortable when you first meet someone because you are so shy. I was interested in that because we just met one another today. I have experienced you as outgoing and confident.
- You mentioned that you want to do everything you can to make the basketball team. You also said you haven't had time to go to practice this week because you were going out with your boyfriend every night. That doesn't seem to fit.
- I want to check something out with you. It seems like you have many reservations about this relationship. And yet you keep trying to figure out ways to be around Kay.
- I invite you to think about something between now and when we talk again in a couple days. You've talked so much about wanting to be a physician. Yet you have told me you don't like to be around sick people. You feel sick to your stomach when you see blood. You don't like science, and you're really anxious to start earning a living.

Challenging is an important part of our work as professional helpers. However, we need to challenge with messages and expressions that our students clients can receive without becoming immobilized with defensiveness. We must also remain alert to their reactions, which may not be expressed verbally. Because students regularly encounter disciplinary actions, adult redirection, and evaluation in schools, school counselors and school psychologists must offer challenges without sounding punitive or judgmental.

Effective challenges are predicated on solid working relationships, appropriate timing, and thoughtful language. Effective helpers model congruence between verbal and nonverbal communication, particularly when challenging. They actively attend to students' responses to their challenges and respond accordingly.

Tour Guide Note: In the following interchange, the school counselor (SC) balances her challenging response with reflections of content and meaning. The SC also gauges Jill's receptivity to challenges.

Jill: I just have to pass! It would be awful. I will do anything I need to so I can go to seventh grade.

SC: It sounds like you're worried that you won't pass, and you're feeling desperate.

Jill: I'm not worried, because I know I will pass because I absolutely have to.

SC: You're convinced that you will do what you need to do because passing is so important to you [*silence*].

SC: I'm confused. Perhaps it would help if you told me more about what prompted you to come today, and also explain how important it is for you to pass.

Jill: I just talked with Mr. Jellian and he told me I was in grade trouble because I have missed too many classes.

SC: Now you're worried that you're not going to pass because you haven't been going to class regularly.

Jill: I'm not wasting time on going to his classes. I don't need to be in class to learn about what's going on. I can pass the tests without being bored to death in his stupid classes.

SC: You don't like going to the classes, and you're confident you can pass the tests even though you don't go. I just want to mention something that doesn't seem to fit. When you first came in you mentioned that you would do anything to pass so you can go to seventh grade, yet it doesn't sound like you're willing to go to class.

It is important to remember the purpose of challenging. As discrepancies are made explicit, awareness is increased. Awareness of personal inconsistency can promote change. Challenging is another way of holding a metaphoric mirror to increase students' self-awareness, which Gladding defined as "an ongoing *process* in life of recognizing thoughts, emotions, senses, and behaviors that influence a person on multiple levels" (2006, p. 128).

Think about a young person about whom you care—perhaps a son or daughter, a niece or nephew, the child of a friend. Imagine that he or she engages in behavior that you think is self-defeating in some way. With that situation in mind, compose a challenging statement that would not compromise respect or jeopardize the relationship.

_____

_____

_____

_____

INTERPRETATION

Interpretation is sometimes considered a negative term that conjures images of lying on a couch while a bearded, pipe-smoking analyst "interprets" every thought and action. We use the term in a broad manner to reflect the process of introducing a new way of understanding an issue. These types of interventions go beyond what the student client has explicitly stated and introduce "a new meaning, reason or explanation for behaviors, thoughts, or feelings so that clients can see problems in a new way" (Hill, 2004, p. 245). Interpretations can take various forms and include

- making connections between statements or events that do not appear to be related (e.g., "I know we've talked about how much pressure you're feeling from home, school, and your friends. I'm wondering how that might connect to what happened today when you 'blew your top' at Ms. Kennedy.")
- pointing out themes or patterns in a student's behaviors, thoughts, or feelings (e.g., "It seems like you get really angry when people try to tell you what to do, like your stepdad, your teachers, and even your friends do. I wonder what it means to you when people tell you what to do.")
- offering a new framework for understanding behaviors, thoughts, feelings, or problems (e.g., "You say that you don't really care what your parents think, but you've described a lot of situations when you've really tried to get their attention.")

> After providing an interpretation, allow time for reflection. Silence is an effective tool to help you and the student client decide where to go next.

Before offering an interpretation, professionals should ensure that rapport has been established. Further, they need to watch for signs that student clients are ready to look at themselves at a deeper level.

Let's take the example of **Ruth**, a junior in high school who cried, "I just don't know why I get so mad at my parents. I know they care about me and are just trying to protect me. I get so mad and I end up saying horrible things that I feel so bad about later on."

In this instance, Ruth is clearly stating a desire for more understanding of her reactions and is quite distressed at her current responses. A helper's response might be, "You feel guilty when you become angry at your parents, and you're trying to figure out why it is you get so mad at them. Perhaps if you could figure that out, you'd find a way to change the pattern."

For other students clients, interpretation might not work. They may simply want to know how to change their behavior as opposed to why it occurs in the first place. Interpretations should be delivered in a gentle, tentative manner, and the helper should attend to the student clients' reactions to the interpretive statements (Hill, 2004). Furthermore, interpretation is another skill that should be used sparingly in any one session. The example below provides different formats as well as different levels of interpretation.

Jose, a senior: I hate Arturo. Today when I was outside waiting for the bell to ring, he started pickin' at me. Just sort of diggin' at me. Sometimes he's okay, but then he starts in and makes these comments like, "I saw Julia with Roberto the other day," when he knows that Julia and I just broke up. He tells me about a great party that I wasn't invited to. It just seems like it's all the time and I get so mad at him, I want to hit him. It's always right about then that a teacher comes up and I'm the one who gets in trouble.

When you're around Arturo you get in trouble because you lose control (tentative).

Arturo pushes your buttons by bringing up things that have been hurtful or difficult for you (direct).

Could it be that you feel defensive and lose control when someone talks about situations when you've felt hurt or vulnerable? (more direct).

As you watch a movie, video, or television program (or even read a novel), watch for opportunities to venture interpretations. Think about interpretations that would likely be plausible and that you think the person would be able to accept without feeling the need to defend him or herself. With the safety of the screen or printed page, try a few!

REFLECTING MEANING

Reflecting meaning that individuals assign to events and situations is an advanced level of empathy. As we become more attuned to student clients' perceptions and views of the world as well as their immediate environment, we are able to grasp themes and meanings they attribute to experiences. For example, a high school counselor might say, "I just had a thought I'd like to check out with you. Last week you talked about shooting free throws during the tournament. You also mentioned that you got an 88 or 89 on several tests. This week we have talked about your ACT scores that were a bit lower than you had hoped. A theme I keep hearing relates to just missing the mark by one or two points."

Deeper meanings are also explicated as professionals communicate their understanding of student clients' internal experiences. In this regard, Combs and Gonzalez (1994) remarked that "concentration of attention on the person's meaning is characteristic of effective helpers in all branches of the helping professions" (p. 171). Welch (1998) offered a stronger description:

> The language of facts and data is bland. It is unseasoned. In comparison, the language of meaning, emotion, and significance is peppered with allusions to consequences in the life of the person. An attentive psychotherapist listens to a person's word selection in telling the story. The language of turmoil is dramatic, emotional, metaphoric, and symbolic. . . . To the educated ear of a psychotherapist the language of turmoil reveals connections that might be unknown to the person seeking therapy. (p. 35)

Culture, values, previous experiences, parental influences, and other dynamic forces converge around the meaning assigned to any situation at any given time. Thus, reflecting meaning can be difficult. Because meaning is often communicated implicitly, effective professionals rely on other basic skills, such as reflection of affect and facilitative inquiry, to gain insight about the meaning various experiences and situations have for the individual. They also make inferences based on intuition and their own experiences. Please don't discount or dismiss your intuition. As you gain experience, we hope you will pay attention to your "informed gut."

> Tour Guide Note: Notice how the school counselor (SC) invites Chi-Chen to explore deeper levels of meaning by reflecting his implied message and affect.

Chi-Chen: I can't believe it. I just found out last night that I didn't make the ACT cut off score, so I won't be able to go to CU. It's the only place I want to go. It's the only place I even applied. They must have made a mistake. I can't believe they'd be so stupid! I've got to figure out what happened.

SC: You're angry about this. You're feeling desperate and trapped because you wanted to go to CU so much you hadn't even considered the possibility of going somewhere else.

Chi-Chen: Never. I don't *want* to go anywhere else. My mom went to CU. My dad went to CU. My sister went to CU. My friends are at CU. I *have* to go to CU.

SC: Not only is it important for you to attend CU, it sounds like it is important to lots of other people.

Chi-Chen: Yes. My parents are expecting me to go to CU. That's just what we all do.

SC: It's as if you would be letting your parents down if you didn't go to CU.

Chi-Chen: Well, yeah. I don't even want to tell them about this.

SC: I have a hunch I want to check out with you. When you first came in, you seemed angry. You were sure a mistake had been made. Now you seem more embarrassed, or perhaps ashamed, because you think you will disappoint your parents.

Again, as you watch a movie, video, or television program or read a novel, watch for opportunities to reflect what might be core meanings. Take advantage of the safety of the screen or printed page to rehearse advanced empathic responses.

CONFRONTING OUR OWN CHALLENGES
RELATED TO ADVANCED SKILLS

Our preservice school counselors and school psychologists sometimes express anxiety that they will reflect inaccurately or offensively if they extend their responses beyond the words they hear. Actually, it is better to risk deeper level empathic responses and be wrong than to remain at a shallow level of reflecting and concluding that "empathy doesn't work" (a comment we have heard from preservice professionals before they learned to reflect with accuracy). Professional self-efficacy and willingness to risk with student clients is sometimes referred to as a *use of self*.

What does the notion of use of self mean to you? How can you use yourself when you're absorbed in composing reflections, avoiding questions, and trying to figure out what the other person and the supervisor wants from you?

Though the composition of our reflections and the style of our questions are important, the relationships we develop are the most important factor in our ability to be helpful. Your comfort with the various skills will contribute to your ability to be genuine and to use your inherent and unique therapeutic qualities.

Indeed, the skills you are learning are important, but you must also attend to the unique presence that you alone can bring to the counseling relationship. Basic skills facilitate solid working relationships. Advanced skills help student clients increase understanding of themselves, and move forward with changes that will improve their lives. We refer to the presence of a solid working relationship as *engagement*. By consistently demonstrating respect, authenticity, and empathy, effective school counselors and school psychologists communicate their willingness to engage in a professional relationship. As student clients respond to the invitational environment, they become willing to engage in the process of counseling, to feel vulnerable, and to struggle with difficult issues.

RESPECTING CULTURAL DIFFERENCES

We have focused on basic and advanced counseling skills as well as respect, authenticity, empathy, and engagement. Cultural responsiveness does not preclude any of these qualities. However, their expressions may differ somewhat as competent professionals work with children and youth from diverse backgrounds. For example, many aspects of nonverbal communication are culturally embedded. Children and youth from some ethnic groups may be less comfortable with eye contact. Questions may be counterproductive with groups who are less comfortable disclosing personal information. Leaning forward may be experienced as aggression or intrusion.

Do culturally responsive professionals avoid these behaviors then? Not necessarily. Instead, culturally sensitive professional helpers proceed with an attitude of respect and appreciation that allows students and parents to teach them how to best work together. They may find it helpful to use immediacy or self-disclosure to invite conversations about the cultural differences; such dialogue in the safety of a counseling (or consultation) relationship may help individuals from nondominant cultural backgrounds understand their peers and teachers. For example, a school psychologist working with a student client who has recently immigrated might say, "Your school in Guatemala must be different from our school in Montgomery. Sometimes, I worry that you aren't comfortable when we talk about your schedule and jobs you're trying to find because I'm white and I've never lived in Guatemala. In fact, I've always lived in Alabama. My life is much easier than yours is right now." Such disclosure may invite the student to explore cultural differences and learn about his or her impact on relationships and adjustment to the new environment.

With a partner, if possible, practice using responses to these scenarios that demonstrate immediacy, self-disclosure, challenging, and interpretation. Additionally, consider core meanings that the student might be communicating. Provide each other feedback.

You have just begun to work with Mallory, a 9-year-old girl who consistently complains about anxiety before tests. You are confused because Mallory does well on tests. You don't think you fully understand Mallory's experience.

Mallory: Whenever I have to take tests, my stomach starts to hurt. I'm so stupid and I hate tests!

Immediacy:

_____

_____

_____

Challenge:

_____

_____

_____

Self-disclosure:

_____

_____

_____

Interpretation:

_____

_____

_____

Possible core meaning:

_____

_____

_____

Eduardo, a 7-year-old boy, has had trouble making friends in his new school. Sometimes, his frustration is expressed through aggressive comments. You have also discovered references to problems with peer relationships from the previous school's cumulative record. Eduardo seeks you out two to three times a week, and his relationship with you may be the most prominent relationship he has in the school. Eduardo is a member of a group you lead for second grade boys; however, he does not attend regularly.

Eduardo: Everyone picks on me. They call me names and won't play with me. This school is stupid! I want to go back to my old school.

Immediacy:

_____

_____

_____

Challenge:

_____

_____

_____

Self-disclosure:

_____

_____

_____

Interpretation:

_____

_____

_____

Elias, a 14-year-old male, has the potential of being a strong student. Even though he has expressed his desire to achieve higher grades, his performance is inconsistent. You have worked with Elias in classroom activities, and he has participated in a study skills group you led. During the group, he indicated that he would care about schoolwork if he knew how he'd use what he learns as an adult. He does not have any career plans; you have asked him to participate in a career exploration group you plan to start.

Elias: I don't want to be in another group. I'll just find a job. School sucks! We don't learn anything useful and everyone there is stuck up. I don't see why I have to go.

Immediacy:

_____

_____

_____

Challenge:

_____

_____

_____

Self-disclosure:

_____

_____

_____

Interpretation:

_____

_____

_____

Possible core meaning:

_____

_____

_____

Cowles (1997) suggested that

> an effective counseling relationship creates a unique kind of intimacy. In the brief counseling period, the counselor opens self to the experience of another in all its intensity and encounters the paradox of attending to the other by attending to self. It is the essence of assuming the "as if" position. While in the world of the client, the counselor is in the presence of his or her own anxiety: fear, anger, and despair. . . . Such intimacy is frightening and requires great courage. (p. 58)

As you read this paragraph, what thoughts go through your mind?

_____

_____

_____

_____

_____

Think about a time when you felt vulnerable. Consider your own personal pain or childhood experiences that may contribute to your own vulnerability in a counseling session.

_____

_____

_____

_____

_____

What will you do to recognize your anxiety or feelings of vulnerability and separate your experience from that of the student clients or adults with whom you work?

_____

_____

_____

_____

_____

Cowles (1997) also asserted that "counselors who work with children seem particularly vulnerable to skipping the process of building a relationship with the child client. . . . Perhaps it is because we don't really believe children are capable of depth relationships or because we believe children offer relationship so easily that there is little work to be done to build what is assumed to be already there" (p. 58).

Again, what are your thoughts and reactions to this paragraph?

_____

_____

_____

_____

School-based helpers are often acquainted with all students in their building. What can you do to be sure you don't assume that the relationship is strong enough to proceed?

_____

_____

_____

_____

TOUR 4

Traveling With a Theory

Integration and Personalization

Learning Objectives

- Evaluate theories in terms of their relevance and fit for you
- Consider theories and techniques that you may use to help student clients
- Explore combinations and integration of theories to provide a structure to guide your counseling

Tour Guide Note: Before embarking on this tour, we provide several elements of orientation. Though the tour is not "all about us," we thought it important to share our beliefs about the roles of theories in our work in schools. We also offer suggestions about integrating and adopting theories as meaningful frameworks for counseling children and adolescents in schools. Finally, we provide an outline for case conceptualization.

OUR THEORY ABOUT THEORIES

Theories are pervasive. Indeed, we even have theories about theories. We have several assumptions that inform our theory about theories, which we have listed for you:

1. It is dangerous and professionally irresponsible to provide counseling without articulating a theory that addresses our beliefs about people and about how we can most efficaciously help them change.

2. Useful counseling theories are multidimensional, addressing (a) beliefs about human nature, (b) values and opinions regarding happiness and satisfaction, (c) beliefs about mature and well-functioning people, (d) frameworks for conceptualizing and explaining clients' situations, and (e) ideas about how professional helpers facilitate change. Additionally, useful theories have empirical support.

3. We can't *not* have a theory. Counseling does not exist without a theory.

When mental health professionals neglect the important work of defining theories that inform their work, they run the risk of imposing the implicit theories that guide their lives—based on their own experiences as children or as adults. As I (S.M.) often told my students, the Magnusonion theory has not stood the test of time; nor has it been scrutinized in professional arenas. To prevent my defaulting to the Magnusonion theory, I must intentionally work from well-respected theories and monitor Magnusonion intrusions (i.e., my own tendencies, opinions, and solutions for solving problems).

Maslow (1965) poignantly addressed professionals' tendency to work from their own frame of reference. Although we would like to include his entire entry in *Humanistic Viewpoints in Psychology* (Severin, 1965, pp. 17–34), we have excerpted a few paragraphs that provide relevant and contemporary challenges to 21st century professionals.

> Everyone, even the year-old child, has a conception of human nature, for it is impossible to live without a theory of how people behave. Every psychologist, however positivistic and anti-theoretical he [or she] may claim to be, nevertheless has a full-blown philosophy of human nature hidden away within him [or her]. It is as if he [or she] guided him [or her] self by a half-known map, which he [or she] disavows and denies, and which is therefore immune to intrusion and correction by newly acquired knowledge. This unconscious map or theory guides his [or her] reactions far more than does his [or her] laboriously acquired experimental knowledge. . . . The issue is not over whether or not to have a philosophy of psychology, *but whether to have one that is conscious or unconscious.* (p. 23)

In many ways, theories resemble road maps. Road maps can be extremely helpful; however, their usefulness is restricted to certain situations. For example, a map of Greeley, Colorado, would not be helpful for someone who is trying to find an office building in Cheyenne, Wyoming. A map of the United States would not be helpful if someone were trying to find a building on the University of Alabama campus in Tuscaloosa. A topographical map would provide little assistance for travelers.

Maps help us organize information such as travel plans. They also help us organize perceptions, but those perceptions are usually limited to one point of view. For example, an aerial map may reflect a different point of view from a highway map or a weather map.

You have heard the adage "The map is not the territory." If we were to stand on a map of a botanical garden, our experience would be nothing compared to the grandeur possible only by visiting the garden. Many times, when people follow a map, they see only the features for which they are looking such as a street sign or a landmark. With this intentional focus, they may miss the richness of nature, the birds, and beautiful trees. Thus, if we were taking a pleasure ride, we might not want to follow a map.

And so it is with counseling theories. Just as there are many kinds of maps, there are many kinds of theories such as career theories, developmental theories, cognitive-behavioral theories, and so forth. To use a theory for the wrong purpose (e.g., using a theory that doesn't match the presenting problem) would not be helpful; in fact, it could be dangerous. The same has already been said for working without following a theory or integration of theories.

INTEGRATION OF THEORIES VERSUS ECLECTICISM

Questions, conversations, and debates regarding combinations of theories have occurred for many years. Some authors and speakers have embraced a philosophy of using one theory exclusively. In the 1960s, Lazarus proposed the integrated BASIC ID (acronym for the modalities of behavior, affective responses, sensory reactions, images, cognitions, interpersonal relationships, and the need for drugs and other biological interventions), which invited a fair amount of controversy. For example, Eysenck (1970) asserted that "an eclectic mixture of all the different methods of therapy . . . would lead us to nothing but a mish-mash of theories, a huggermugger of procedures, a gallimaufry of therapies, and a charivaria of activities having no proper rational, and incapable of being tested" (p. 145). He added that

> what is needed . . . are clear-cut theories leading to specific procedures applicable to specific types of patients; such procedures should be capable of being taught and should also be strictly evaluated for cost-effectiveness. Furthermore, they should be under constant critical scrutiny from the theoretical point of view. Nothing less will do if we are ever to emerge from the present unsatisfactory position where every psychotherapist practices in gloomy silence and solipsistic splendor procedures which he cannot describe, and which have unknown effects, possibly beneficial, possibly harmful, on the patient.

Aside from the amazing vocabulary, what do you think of Eysenck's statements and predictions?

_____

_____

_____

_____

Consider Eysenck's assertions in the context of contemporary challenges regarding evidence-based delivery of services. What, if any, relevance do elements of Eysenck's comments have for contemporary school-based professionals?

_____

_____

_____

_____

What, if any, relevance do elements of Eysenck's comments have for you?

_____

_____

_____

For a fun and light review of theories developed prior to 1993, access Andrew Beale's (1993) "Contemporary Counseling Approaches: A Review for the Practitioner." Maybe you will update Dr. Beale's quiz!

INTEGRATION AND PERSONALIZATION

Theory building is a process. Indeed, as school counselors and school psychologists mature and practice, they learn from their students, books and journals they read, conferences they attend, supervision, and various forms of continuing education. In other words, theory building is yet another professional journey without a destination for helping professionals (in all sectors) who commit to lifelong learning and growth.

The first couple miles of that journey may be the most difficult and a time when a map may be most helpful—except, the only map that will work for you is the one *you* create by intentionally integrating established theories to become a workable counseling framework for you in your setting. In this process, preservice professionals often select one primary theory and then incorporate elements from others. They continue to define and refine their orientation as they work with students and clients. With professional maturity, they become adept at designing treatment in response to each student client's unique needs and personality.

We encourage school-based professional helpers to strive toward proficiency in multiple approaches. We are not recommending that you abandon your beliefs, become atheoretical, or work without clarity. Rather, we encourage you to develop a growth plan toward building a broad theoretical repertoire so you will be able to work with versatility.

FACILITATING CHANGE: INITIAL THOUGHTS

Before reading the next section, consider Metcalf's (2008) suggestion that "school counselors [or school psychologists] don't have time to take the scenic route" (p. 45). How does Metcalf's notion compare to Cowles's (1997) ideas that we shared in Tour 3? To what extent do you agree with Metcalf? To what extent do you agree with Cowles?

Sometimes our preservice school counselors and school psychologists become impatient when we focus on basic and advanced skills without addressing strategies to effect change. Once our trainees feel comfortable in their foundational skills, we frequently hear them ask or imply, "Now what?"

Carl Rogers contended that authenticity, unconditional positive regard, and empathic understanding in the context of a solid relationship are "necessary and sufficient conditions" (1957, p. 95) for change. We suggest that they are necessary, sufficient, and appropriate when working with some student clients such as someone who has lost a loved one. There *is* value in simply telling one's story to a responsive, empathic listener.

For other situations such as behavioral or academic problems, we suggest that the conditions described by Rogers are necessary, sufficient, but inefficient. Basic and advanced helping skills create the foundation for the action stage of counseling. That is, once we have built a relationship—achieved engagement—with a student client and collaboratively identified a goal toward which to work, the next step is to select the strategy that will help the student client move toward his or her goal. Cognitive behavioral approaches and several problem solving models offer promising guidance for helping students within the schools.

Thus, a question you must answer is, "How do I help students reach their goals?" That is not a question that is easily answered as it depends on a number of variables. Your essential beliefs about counseling will be reflected in your relationships with children, youth, and adults with whom you work. However, you must also consider (a) what you believe about the etiology of problems, (b) research to support different approaches, and (c) limits of the school setting (e.g., time).

Richard Watts (1993) provided a practical four-phase model for beginning a theory identification and personalization process. Watts's model provides a useful map for this tour.

Personalization Phase One: Exploration of Personal Values and Major Theories

The first "stop" allows time to intentionally consider, identify, and even test your own core beliefs and values. Included in this self-assessment are beliefs about personality development, contributors to problems, empowering events to overcome problems, and professional helpers' roles in facilitating change to overcome problems. Before progressing to the second stop, we also encourage you to consider theories that are most consistent with your personal beliefs.

You have been asked to consider your assumptions about a variety of factors at various junctures of your professional preparation. In fact, we have already asked you to think about your beliefs about children in *Counseling Children and Adolescents in Schools* and in this *Guide*. We've asked you to think about how people change and how school-based professionals facilitate that process. As you become intentional about evaluating various theories related to counseling and gain experience, it will be important to revisit your assumptions—many times. We encourage you to continue the process now with more specificity and more focus.

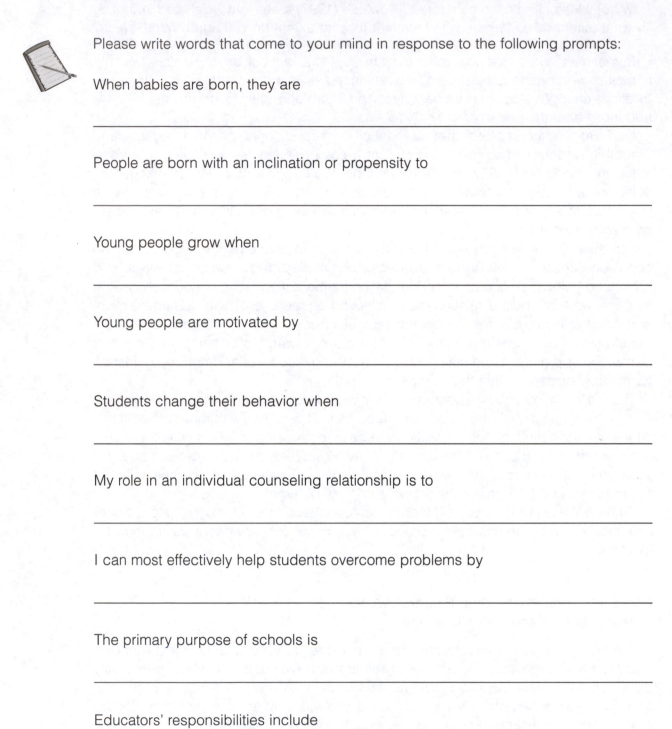

Please write words that come to your mind in response to the following prompts:

When babies are born, they are

_____

People are born with an inclination or propensity to

_____

Young people grow when

_____

Young people are motivated by

_____

Students change their behavior when

_____

My role in an individual counseling relationship is to

_____

I can most effectively help students overcome problems by

_____

The primary purpose of schools is

_____

Educators' responsibilities include

_____

Please write your responses to the following questions with as much specificity (without compromising brevity) as possible:

- What roles do nature and nurture have in the development of young people? (We're not asking for a text book answer—what do *you* think?)

_____

_____

_____

- What motivates students to learn?

_____

_____

_____

- What contributes to psychological, emotional, and mental problems?

_____

_____

_____

- What factors might influence a first or second grade student who refuses to follow adults' directives?

_____

_____

_____

- How should adults respond when a first or second grade student refuses to follow directives repeatedly and throughout the school year?

_____

_____

_____

• What factors contribute to an individual's inability to independently resolve challenges in life?

_____

_____

_____

• To what extent are historical factors relevant to the work you envision as a school-based professional helper?

_____

_____

_____

• How are your personal beliefs and values similar to theories that are most attractive to you?

_____

_____

_____

• Think about 8, 9, or 10 of your most solid values, opinions, and beliefs—related to a variety of personal dimensions (e.g., spiritual, physical, familial). For example, you may believe that the only way we can help children is with child-centered play therapy. You may also believe that divorce is absolutely wrong. You may have strong religious convictions. Undoubtedly, the process of writing your own core beliefs and values will take several days. We encourage you to begin writing now. We will revisit the process and encourage you to continue it long after our time with you is over.

_____

_____

_____

_____

_____

_____

_____

_____

_____

_____

_____

_____

_____

You have already studied a variety of theories. We have reviewed several of them in *Counseling Children and Adolescents in Schools*. You probably have read about others that are particularly interesting to you. At this point, which three or four theories come the closest to making sense to you, fitting with your core beliefs, and providing guidance for your work with children and adolescents in schools?

_____

_____

_____

_____

Authors have provided useful questionnaires that guide preservice professionals' initial steps toward selecting primary theories on which to base their work (e.g., the Selective Theory Sorter, Revised, Halbur & Halbur, 2011, pp. 27–31). Responses to and results of these instruments sometimes surprise preservice professionals and increase their self-understanding.

Personalization Phase Two: Examination of One or Two Theories

Your next stop features focused selection, inquiry, study, and examination of a few theories. The process may result in cycling back and forth between this and the previous stops.

This is not a task that can be completed easily in one academic term. While you have access to university libraries, we encourage you to identify original texts that you can read in time; for example, if you like client-centered approaches, read a few books by Rogers. If you feel comfortable with cognitive approaches, read books written by Ellis, Beck, or Meichenbaum.

For now, begin to narrow your thinking to the aspects of theories you like and that you believe will be useful to you as you work with student clients. How might you draw from the two or three theories you like best? What techniques will you use? How can you reconcile essential differences in the theories?

_____

_____

_____

_____

Personalization Phase Three: Integration

Rarely do school-based professionals rely on one theory. Indeed, one theory is not appropriate or helpful for every counseling situation. Additionally, each theory can be augmented with techniques drawn from other approaches. Thus, professionals integrate theories.

During this stop, it is important for you to consider internal consistency. In other words, is there adequate agreement in the combined approaches to be effectively used in combination? For example, if you are convinced that early childhood experiences are primary components of behavior, choice theory would not be sufficient for you. However, you might combine elements of choice theory with individual psychology (Adler).

Personalization Phase Four: Personalization!

Our final stop (for now) is personalization. As a school counselor or a school psychologist, you bring your unique personality and interactive style to each counseling relationship you encounter. As you become acquainted with your professional roles and with various theories, you will have many opportunities to integrate the theories, your experiences, and your personality into a meaningful, authentic style of counseling.

Watts (1993) emphasized, as we do, that the process of theory building, integration, and personalization continues throughout each professional helper's career.

Clarity, refinement, depth of understanding, versatility, and personal development are cyclic and dynamic. Intentionality and investment in the process contribute to professional maturity and excellence.

As you consider the theories that seem most congruent with your values, beliefs, personality, and counseling style think about issues and students with whom you will work. For whom is your constructed theory most appropriate?

_____

_____

_____

For which students or situations will you need to modify your preferred approaches? (For example, you may feel comfortable with cognitive and behavioral theories, or with reality therapy. What modifications might be necessary for working with a student client whose parents died in an accident?)

_____

_____

_____

We introduced Cassie and Hans in *Counseling Children and Adolescents in Schools*. We asked you to consider information you would need to help them. Throughout the chapters, we illustrated conceptualization through a single lens, or through one theory. As you think about them now, and the various theories from which you could work, what approaches seem most relevant or useful for each of them?

Hans:

_____

Cassie:

_____

Assuming you were working with Hans or Cassie, how might you integrate theories and draw from various techniques to help them?

Hans:

_____

_____

Cassie:

_____

_____

> As we near the end of this tour, we hope you will begin to metaphorically pack your repertoire of theory-based techniques and strategies for working with students—in a systematic way that will help you with retrieval. You may consider theories that make sense for helping children in transitions or theories that seem useful for student clients who have lost loved ones. You may find another category for students having difficulty with motivation.

We also encourage you to consider a nonmetaphoric filing system for techniques and modalities (e.g., play and group). Although we haven't elaborated on techniques and interventions, we encourage you to investigate and try several. We have begun a list of interventions and atheoretical techniques. We encourage you to think about how they would be consistent with or appropriate for incorporation within your preferred theories (Figure 4.1).

Figure 4.1 Counseling Techniques and Strategies

Counseling with toys
Counseling with board games
Counseling with cooperative games
Counseling with art
Adventure-based counseling
Storytelling
Mutual storytelling
Metaphors in counseling
Externalization (from Narrative Therapy)
Therapeutic letters
Bibliotherapy
Video-based counseling
Incomplete sentence activities
Empty chair (Gestalt)
Role playing
Motivational interviewing
Puppetry
Music therapy
Dance therapy
Equine therapy
Animal-assisted therapy
Using sand trays and miniature figures in counseling

TOUR 5

Facilitating Change

Conceptualization, Planning, Progress Monitoring, and Documentation

Learning Objectives

- Learn essential elements of case conceptualization
- Apply case conceptualization to the process of outlining a plan for counseling
- Identify strategies for monitoring progress
- Practice documentation

By this juncture of your journey, you have likely identified a theory or elements of a few theories that you particularly like. You also have a general knowledge of other theories, and you are beginning to accumulate a repertoire of theory-based interventions. Despite your preferences, however, it will be important to consider the needs of each student with whom you work as you determine how you will work with him or her (Berman, 2010). This process is called *case conceptualization*.

Conceptualization guides professionals in accurately identifying problems, factors that contribute to problems, resources for resolving those problems, and strategies for assisting in the resolution of the problems. Monitoring progress creates a feedback loop for student clients and professionals who work with them. Documentation contributes to continuity. The combination of conceptualization, planning, progress monitoring, and documentation contributes to unified, internally consistent, coherent work with individual students or groups. You will have opportunities to increase your awareness of these elements of professional practice on this tour. We begin with an illustration of case conceptualization within the context of consultation.

A few years ago, I (S.M.) was asked to conduct a functional behavior assessment (FBA) for an elementary child (whose name will be Bobbi for this illustration). The principal's primary concerns related to disruptive behavior and defiant responses to adults' redirections. Even though I was in the role of consultant, I followed case conceptualization procedures. I carefully documented each step I took during observation and conceptualization just as I would have if I were providing direct services.

I observed Bobbi and her classmates during spelling, handwriting, math, and music. I also observed as the teacher read to the students. I attended to teachers' actions, classmates' responses, and Bobbi's behaviors. All together, I was with Bobbi and her class for approximately 3 hours. I also asked teachers to complete a questionnaire that included an item that was repeated three times: "When Bobbi _____ I felt _____."

I returned to my office and endeavored to make sense of the various behaviors and interactions I had observed. I "tried on" a variety of theoretical lenses, hoping to find an explanation that would lead to interventions—plausible hypotheses that I could present during a meeting with teachers, the counselor, the school nurse, and the principal.

I began thinking from an Adlerian perspective and asked myself several questions. What could the goals of Bobbi's behavior be? Is she seeking undue attention? Is she trying to get power? Could it be that she is seeking revenge? Does she have relationships with adults and peers? What about natural or logical consequences? Does she perceive herself as capable? What about courage?

My response to the last question captured my attention. "This kid is not afraid of anything!" This was a poignant reminder to bracket and monitor my own reactions.

I returned to possible goals of Bobbi's behavior. Could her behavior be related to attention? I didn't think so. Based on teachers' responses to Bobbi's actions and a variety of things that she had said, I considered possibilities of power seeking strategies. I observed that she had made an irrelevant, though potentially hurtful, comment to a guest who was leading an activity the children obviously enjoyed. When I mentioned that observation, other adults said Bobbi had made similar comments to them.

Bobbi's grandmother had suggested that Bobbi's behaviors were related to problematic peer relationships. Was Bobbi trying to achieve connections with her peers? Does she perceive herself as having significance in her group? It appeared to me and to the teachers that Bobbi had friends and connections at school. I didn't observe conflict with peers, but I needed to remember the grandmother's hypothesis and guard against discounting it.

I began to think from developmental theories. Bobbi appears to be quite bright, yet she doesn't present the level of maturity we'd expect. She is smaller than her peers. Her behavior doesn't fit what we would expect for moral development. I wondered about her birth and physical development, particularly prior to age 2. Did she learn to trust? Has there been trauma in her life? Could these behaviors be manifestations of prenatal issues? Does she have brothers and sisters? Did she attend preschool? Does the school nurse have information that would be helpful?

That led me to consider biochemical explanations. Could she have attention deficit hyperactivity disorder? What other "medical model" and deficit model explanations could help? With or without pharmacological intervention, we would still need to consider behavioral explanations and interventions. What might occasion behavior? How might we manipulate the environment to shape the behaviors that Bobbi needs to acquire in order to achieve success in school?

As I considered reinforcements and contingencies (from a behavioral perspective), I was perplexed. I reflected on the day and asked myself, "What *does* reinforce this child's behavior? What consequences matter to her? What purposes does her behavior serve? What is the function of Bobbi's behavior?" If I work from a frame that people engage in behaviors for a reason, I need to have a fairly accurate idea about those reasons. Yet what could they be?

And what about exceptions (drawing from solution-focused brief therapy, SFBT)? When *does* she follow instructions? When *does* she complete her work? How will we know that she has overcome these challenges? How will we know we have helped her begin to make progress? What interventions have been tried? Which were successful, or even partially successful? How have we worked with other students with similar behaviors and personalities? If I am able to answer any of these questions, it might provide clues to solutions for helping Bobbi acquire skills for learning as well as interacting with adults and her peers.

As I prepared for the meeting at school, I traced my conceptualization processes and listed questions. Clearly, I needed more information. Yet I was ready to propose a *tentative* hypothesis: The goal of Bobbi's behavior could be power. Within an Adlerian framework, I recommended that the adults at school provide forced choices such as, "You may choose to complete your work at the table with your classmates or you may choose to work at the table in the back of the room," or "You have chosen to sit on the step rather than with your classmates. You may choose to sit on the step and participate or you will choose to go to the office." I suggested that they use this strategy *only* as an experiment with attention to Bobbi's responses. I also asked for more information from the teachers and suggested that the school nurse meet with the parents to explore early childhood developmental factors.

Indeed, this process took time—time that was well invested. As Berman poignantly wrote, the absence of intentional and thoughtful conceptualization may result in "treatment chaos" (2010, p. 2). Without clear understanding of student clients' situations and specifically identified measures of success, professionals run the risk of employing random, incoherent interventions that may not even be appropriate for the presenting problems. It is important to consider many aspects of a student's context in order to develop the best hypotheses. In other words, you must "complicate your thinking." Rather than relying on one preferred explanation (e.g., "She must have ADHD"), examine the evidence from multiple perspectives and select the explanation that represents the best fit. Otherwise, your thoughts might reflect something like, "Hm. I'll try [this]. . . . That didn't work. . . . I'll try [this]. . . . Oh. That didn't work. . . . I'll try [this]."

CASE CONCEPTUALIZATION

The process of matching your understanding of student clients' issues with your own theory of human behavior is referred to as *case conceptualization*. Together, these two elements help you decide on a strategy or plan for helping student clients achieve their goals. When possible, professionals should implement empirically supported treatment methods for these presenting issues. Unfortunately, most of the strategies supported in the research have focused on specific clinical issues (e.g., anxiety, depression, or conduct disorders) rather than more general difficulties (e.g., coping with parental divorce, struggling with peer friendships). Additionally, professionals must consider broader aspects of the school environment to determine whether the selected strategies are realistic, appropriate for school-based intervention, and feasible given time availability and time restraints. Shorter term, problem solving approaches are generally recommended for school-based professional helpers, even though other approaches may inform your thinking about students and the situations they encounter.

Conceptualization is a problem solving process, a comprehensive examination of factors related to the current difficulties and possibilities for their resolution. As Mennuti, Freeman, and Christner (2006, p. 38) suggested,

> case conceptualization is a dynamic and efficient way to capture the multifaceted issues presented by each child or adolescent. From this process flows an individualized intervention or treatment plan that accounts for the child's cognitive, affective and behavioral functioning, while simultaneously considering cultural and familial context as well as developmental level. An accurate case conceptualization provides the clinician with detailed information about the child's past behavior, explains current behavior, and allows for prediction of future behavior.

Thus, conceptualization includes a concise identification of the presenting problem, consideration of the etiology and history of the situation, goals, and procedures for facilitating the attainment of those goals. In this process, attention is given to development, culture, context, school performance, behavior, family dynamics, relevant history, and resources. Factors that contribute to or maintain the problem are identified. Hypotheses regarding resolution of the situation are generated. Professional helpers consider what theories provide the most useful explanation for the situation as well as a potential sequence of treatment.

Ultimately, an internally consistent, yet flexible, plan for helping student clients resolve challenges is designed. Briefly, this is a process of answering three questions: (a) How did this person get into this situation? and (b) What is his or her ticket out? Responses to those questions will guide the answer to (c), How can I most effectively and efficiently help?

Tour Guide Note: A high school student, Daryl, will accompany you on this tour. In fact, you will be working with him (albeit theoretically and indirectly).

Daryl is a 17-year-old high school junior. He has had an individualized educational plan (IEP) since he was in sixth grade. He is currently scheduled to work with a special education teacher in the resource room 2 hours a day, which he enjoys because he has a close connection with this teacher. Daryl attends classes and has modified assignments. He participates in school activities such as drama and has been active in track and other sports. However, he recently discontinued all athletic activities because of problems with asthma.

Daryl lives with his mother and father. He has no brothers or sisters. Daryl's mother is a school librarian (at Daryl's school). His father is a disabled veteran.

Daryl began to complain about stomach pains during the fall academic term and missed several days of school, particularly morning classes. During winter break, his mother consulted with their family physician, who provided a diagnosis of generalized anxiety disorder. Because the physician could not identify medical explanations for Daryl's physical pain, he recommended individual counseling with a focus on stress management.

Daryl's mother requested assistance from his special education teacher, who consulted with the special education team. In collaboration with Daryl and his mother, the team requested that you arrange to work with Daryl during a sequence of eight individual counseling sessions.

Assume a professional helper who works solely from individual psychology (i.e., Adler's theory) learned about Daryl. What questions might he or she raise? What hypotheses might he or she generate?

_____

_____

_____

_____

Assume a professional helper who works solely from cognitive-behavioral approaches learned about Daryl. What questions might he or she raise? What hypotheses might he or she generate?

_____

_____

_____

_____

Assume an SFBT-based professional helper works with Daryl. What questions might he or she raise? What hypotheses might he or she generate?

_____

_____

_____

_____

Assume a reality therapy-based professional helper works with Daryl. What questions might he or she raise? What hypotheses might he or she generate?

_____

_____

_____

_____

What questions seem pertinent to you? What initial hypotheses do you have?

_____

_____

_____

_____

_____

What steps will you take in preparation for your first session with Daryl?

_____

_____

_____

_____

With the limited information that you have, what priorities will you establish for the first session? What will your goals for the first session include?

_____

_____

_____

Your First Session With Daryl

Questions from the Tour Guides: Where are you and Daryl meeting? How is the room arranged? Where do you sit? Where does Daryl sit? What does Daryl look like? How is he dressed? What is his demeanor? Your observations of Daryl and experiences as you work with him are important factors to consider in the conceptualization and planning process.

Daryl explains that his stomach pains occur primarily in the morning and to the extent that he cannot eat before noon. He says that he sometimes comes to school just before lunch, which he likes to have at school so he can visit with his friends. Daryl indicates that he has a few friends. He emphasizes that having friends is the most important thing in his life.

Daryl tells you that he is way behind in his classes and he dreads coming to school. He complains about interpersonal problems with a few of his teachers and also about being teased by some of his classmates.

Daryl discusses problems with his family. His father's experiences in the military resulted in a traumatic brain injury and post–traumatic stress disorder (PTSD) symptoms. His mother has a history of medical challenges as well. Daryl describes a much closer relationship with his mother than with his father. He also says that he worries about both of his parents but particularly about his mother.

Daryl also tells you that he experienced depression and sometimes contemplated suicide during the previous year. Daryl's mother took him to an emergency room during the summer break; however, the professionals who conducted the assessment did not believe hospitalization was warranted.

Question from the Tour Guides: How will you respond to Daryl's conversation about previous suicidal ideation?

The following dialogue is taken from the concluding moments of the first session:

You: I'd like to get a better understanding of your level of stress right now, as you experience it. Let's imagine that 1 means no stress. You don't have a care in the world. You aren't worried about anything. Your stomach feels fine. You're eating anything you want at any time of the day. That's 1. 10 would be lots of stress. You feel so stressed that when someone comes up behind you in the hall, you jump. Your stomach feels so awful that you cannot even imagine eating. You are worried to the point you can't sleep. You try to come to school and you can't even function. That's 10. What rating would you say you had this morning when you came to school?

Daryl: This morning? Maybe 8.

You: What about right now?

Daryl: Probably 6.

You: What did you do between the time when you came to school and now to bring that down to 6?

Daryl: What did I do? Nothing. It just happened.

You: Well, I think you had more to do with it than you're giving yourself credit for [smiling to maintain the relationship], but we'll talk about that later. We will be working together for the next seven weeks. Let's pretend that we're already to our last session rather than our first, and that our work has been really helpful for you. In fact, when I ask you to rate your level of stress, you say it is at 3. What will be happening that week so you will rate your experience of stress at 3?

Daryl: I'll be more myself.

You: Okay. I don't know you well enough to know what that means, so let's say I'm out in the hallway or even visiting your classes. What will I see you doing so I will know that you are more yourself?

Daryl: I'll be talking more with my friends and not just hanging around by myself.

You: [*nodding*] What else will you be doing when you are more yourself?

Daryl: I'll be more successful.

You: And what will your friends and teachers notice when you are more successful?

Daryl: I'll make decisions about doing my work and going to school on my own. Adults won't have to make me do stuff and nag at me all the time. Mom won't be on my case.

You: Hmm. What else?

Daryl: I don't know. Maybe my stomach won't hurt as much.

You: So you'll talk with your friends more. You'll be in charge of doing your work without adults bothering you about it. And your stomach will feel better. I'm wondering what you'll do so everyone will know that your stomach no longer hurts.

So that gives us some ideas about what you'll be doing when our work has been helpful for you. Let's back that up. Let's say that when you come back next week, and I ask you to rate your stress, you say it is 5-1/2, down just 1/2 notch from today. What will be some things that will happen throughout the week so you will say it is 5-1/2 rather than 6?

Daryl: Maybe I'll come to school. But I don't think that's going to happen.

You: Remember, I said down just 1/2 notch, not down to 3 or 4.

Daryl: I'd probably be here most of the afternoons and a couple of the mornings.

You: What else?

Daryl: I don't know. Maybe I'll catch up a little bit with my homework.

You: Which teachers will notice the change first?

Daryl: Mr. Joe. Maybe Ms. Teresa.

You: I'm wondering if you'd be willing to do a homework assignment for me—and I'll be the only adult who knows about it.

Daryl: [*noncommittally shrugs his shoulders*]

You: I'd like you to pay close attention to what's going on the days when you rate your stress level below 7. It doesn't have to be below 7 all day long because I have an idea it's a bit higher in the morning and during a couple of your tougher classes. Just pay attention to what happens when it's 7. Okay?

Daryl: Okay.

You: See you next week? [*Daryl nods in agreement.*] Do you want me to come get you, or will you just come down on your own?

Daryl: I don't want you to come get me. I'll come down.

Assume you are a professional helper who works solely from individual psychology. What will you consider as you plan your work with Daryl? What interventions might you use? What priorities will you establish for the next session? What will you need to do prior to the next session?

_____

_____

_____

_____

Assume you are a professional helper who works solely from cognitive-behavioral approaches. What will you consider as you plan your work with Daryl? What interventions might you use? What priorities will you establish for the next session? What will you need to do prior to the next session?

_____

_____

_____

_____

Assume you are an SFBT-based professional helper. What will you consider as you plan your work with Daryl? What interventions might you use? What priorities will you establish for the next session? What will you need to do prior to the next session?

_____

_____

_____

_____

Assume you are a reality therapy–based professional helper. What will you consider as you plan your work with Daryl? What interventions might you use? What priorities will you establish for the next session? What will you need to do prior to the next session?

_____

_____

_____

_____

What questions seem pertinent to you? What initial hypotheses do you have?

_____

_____

_____

_____

What do you think might be standing between Daryl and his idea of "being more himself" and "being successful"? Which theory, or combination of theories, provides the most plausible and useful set of lenses through which you can view Daryl's situation?

_____

_____

_____

What elements of that approach are particularly apropos?

_____

_____

_____

Which approaches provide promising strategies for guiding interventions you will use and for helping Daryl overcome his challenges?

_____

_____

_____

Prior to the second session, you have several tasks, which may include the following:

- Documenting the first session
- Reviewing school records (You may have done this before the first session.)
- Interviewing or consulting with teachers (You may have done this before the first session.)
- Interviewing or consulting with parents (You may have done this before the first session.)
- Drafting goals for your work
- Drafting plans for your work (sometimes called treatment planning)

As you consider Daryl's situation and the things he reported during his first counseling session, what do you anticipate will be logical goals? In other words, how do *you* hope Daryl will be different at the conclusion of the 8 weeks during which he works with you? How will you arrive at the goals? What goals and language will most likely be acceptable, even invitational, to Daryl? With goals in mind, how will you work toward their attainment?

Tour Guide Note: In Table 5.1, we have provided a comprehensive conceptualization guide adapted from the models of Murphy and Christner (2006) and Neufeldt, Iversen, and Juntunen (1995). Indeed, school-based professionals may not always have the time required for responding to each element of conceptualization. Additionally, some components may not be relevant or necessary for determining how to most effectively help each student client with whom we work. At the same time, attention to the various elements of the form ensures that important information is not overlooked.

Table 5.1 Case Conceptualization Guide

Student's name: _____ Date: _____

Student's age: _____

Significant adults: _____

Presenting concerns: _____

_____

_____

_____

_____

_____

Category(ies) of concerns:

_____ Behavior

_____ Career decision making

_____ Postsecondary planning

_____ Academic

_____ Relationship conflict

_____

_____

(Note: The presenting problem guides direction of conceptualization. For example, career indecision is related to career theory. Relationship problems could indicate the need for interpersonal skill building. Behavior problems may be a sign of limited skills, unmet needs, or distorted perceptions.)

Student's perception/explanation of the concerns:

_____

_____

_____

_____

_____

Teachers' perception/explanation of the concerns:

_____

_____

_____

_____

Significant adults' perception/explanation of the concerns:

_____

_____

_____

_____

Professional helper's perception/explanation of the concerns:

_____

_____

_____

_____

(Continued)

Table 5.1 (Continued)

Relevant history (relevant to the situation and the school):

Grades:

_____

Attendance:

_____

Behavior patterns:

_____

Other factors:

_____

_____

_____

_____

Potential factors that contribute to maintenance of the presenting concern (e.g., secondary gains):

_____

_____

_____

_____

Hypotheses regarding resolution:

_____ Learn new behavior or change a behavior

_____ Change perceptions or belief system

_____ Develop insight and awareness

_____ Factual information

_____ Encouragement

_____

_____

Student's assets:

_____

_____

_____

_____

Student's abilities, talents, and strengths:

_____

_____

_____

_____

Possible resources:

_____

_____

_____

_____

(Continued)

Table 5.1 (Continued)

Developmental factors (e.g., cognitive, psychosocial):

_____

_____

_____

_____

Relevant cultural, ethnic, economic, contextual factors:

_____

_____

_____

_____

Relevant theories and approaches:

_____

_____

_____

_____

Helping strategies that seem most plausible to me:

_____

_____

_____

_____

Helping strategies that may be acceptable to the student:

_____

_____

_____

_____

Mutually agreed upon goals:

_____

_____

_____

_____

Initial plan: (Note: Consider who will be involved, modalities, and level of intervention):

_____

_____

_____

_____

With the information you have for Daryl, begin to complete the conceptualization form (Table 5.1). Based on what you do know, take creative license to anticipate entries for which you don't have information.

Defining Goals

Conceptualization provides a foundation for planning the work you will do with Daryl. Counseling is more profitable when student clients, their professional helpers, and other significant adults agree on the goals and plans. Thus, we encourage you to take a collaborative stance, regardless of the theories that guide your work.

The crafting of goals warrants investment in terms of thought and time. You may initially prepare a draft that will be approved or modified by the student client or others. Goals should be framed in student clients' language when possible. They should be specific, measurable, achievable, realistic, and timely.

Educators often refer to **SMART** goals, which are

Specific

Measurable

Achievable and **A**ctive

Realistic, **R**esults oriented, and **R**elevant

Timely

Sometimes, professional helpers incorporate assets with language such as, "I will use my strength(s) of _____ to _____." Other professionals simplify the goal statement with language such as, "Beginning tomorrow and continuing through next Friday, I will _____." Particularly when working with student clients, we recommend having no more than three goals and having them sequenced according to which will be most quickly achieved. Certainly, you may have more than three goals for a student; you can note additional goals and modify your plans as appropriate.

Presenting a written document with goals and progress monitoring can enhance investment for some students. You may find that a format similar to the outline provided in Table 5.2 is helpful for you.

Table 5.2 Action Plan for Goal Setting and Progress Monitoring

The Best High School
Your Town, Your State

DARYL's ACTION PLANNING GUIDE   Date: _____

Goal 1: I will _____

To achieve my goal, I will: _____

_____

Today my rating is: _____   My target date is: _____

PROGRESS LOG:

Date: _____

      1   2   3   4   5   6   7   8   9   10   Objective met!

Notes: _____

_____

_____

Date: _____

      1   2   3   4   5   6   7   8   9   10   Objective met!

Notes: _____

_____

_____

Date: _____

      1   2   3   4   5   6   7   8   9   10   Objective met!

Notes: _____

_____

_____

We particularly like the language and process of SFBT for composing goals. You will notice that influence in our illustrations.

TREATMENT PLANNING

With clear direction defined with goals, your next step is to plan the approach(es), strategies, and interventions you will use. How will you assist the student client in achieving his or her goals? What modalities (e.g., group counseling, parent consultation, teacher consultation, individual counseling) will you include? What interventions do you envision using? To what extent will you address career development?

MONITORING PROGRESS

You have established goals and strategies for achieving those goals. How will you know if your student client is making progress toward those goals? What criteria will you use? You and Daryl already established a 10-point scale to assess his level of stress. To what extent will that be adequate? What other criteria will you consider?

Progress monitoring is a prominent term in education, often connected to response to intervention (RTI). With this emphasis, educators are asked to evaluate the efficacy of each intervention (i.e., teaching strategy) based on students' responses. When something works well, they continue. When something doesn't work, they explore other educational strategies.

School counselors and school psychologists also monitor progress of students with whom they work. Sometimes, that is fairly easy; it can also be challenging. We asked Daryl to scale his level of stress. Even though scaling is a subjective measure that may not be reliable, it is a useful strategy for monitoring progress. Other measures include attendance, grades, completion of work, compliance with expectations, and response to redirection.

Finding measures that are fully objective and timely within a school environment is difficult. Grade point average (GPA) requires information from a variety of sources as well as time to calculate. Previous performance may be included in the calculation. Additionally, difficulty of assignments, the amount of assignments, and other grade-related factors fluctuate. Teachers' responses on rating scales are influenced by their own moods, activities on the school calendar, and classroom group dynamics. Single case design research methods (often based on behavioral theories) are among the many models that are available; however, maintaining tally count procedures is time intensive and not always practical. (See Chapter 13 of *Counseling Children and Adolescents in Schools* for more information on single case design.)

Nonetheless, astute school counselors and school psychologists mitigate challenges and find ways to make data collection feasible, defensible, and helpful. They often use a blend of objective indicators (e.g., attendance and grades) and subjective measures (e.g., self-report ratings and observations).

Check In Check Out (CICO; Crone, Horner, & Hawken, 2010) procedures offer many advantages to professionals in schools. CICO provides instant feedback and reinforcement to students as well as mechanisms for monitoring progress. CICO procedures are established according to each child's needs. Students meet with a designated adult each morning before school and return the record form for the previous day with parents' signatures, prepare a new form, establish goals for the day, discuss strategies for success, and experience encouragement from an invested adult. At the end of each class or time block, CICO students meet with the teacher for less than one minute to discuss ratings. After school, they return to their designated adult to calculate totals and discuss their performance throughout the day. The designated adult documents ratings and writes additional notes for parents on the record form. (An example of a CICO record designed for an elementary student is provided in Table 5.3.)

Table 5.3   Check In Check Out Record

The Best Elementary School

Your Town, Your State

ANN's ACTION PLANNING GUIDE   Date: _____

Plan: Ann will meet with [designated adult] each morning before school and each afternoon right after school. She will take this record form to her parents each evening, and they will sign it. Ann will return it each morning and give it to [designated adult].

	B	**A**	**R**	**K**	
	Be Responsible	Act with Kindness	Respect Others	Keep Safe	
	Do my *best* work	Speak kindly to my classmates	Follow my teachers' instructions	Keep hands and feet to myself	Comments
Literacy	0 1 2 3	0 1 2 3	0 1 2 3	0 1 2 3	
PE	0 1 2 3	0 1 2 3	0 1 2 3	0 1 2 3	
Math	0 1 2 3	0 1 2 3	0 1 2 3	0 1 2 3	
Spanish	0 1 2 3	0 1 2 3	0 1 2 3	0 1 2 3	
Writing	0 1 2 3	0 1 2 3	0 1 2 3	0 1 2 3	
Handwriting	0 1 2 3	0 1 2 3	0 1 2 3	0 1 2 3	
Science/ Social Studies	0 1 2 3	0 1 2 3	0 1 2 3	0 1 2 3	
Library/ Computer	0 1 2 3	0 1 2 3	0 1 2 3	0 1 2 3	
Sign	0 1 2 3	0 1 2 3	0 1 2 3	0 1 2 3	
Music	0 1 2 3	0 1 2 3	0 1 2 3	0 1 2 3	
Art	0 1 2 3	0 1 2 3	0 1 2 3	0 1 2 3	

0 = Reverse observed   1 = Not observed (e.g., no work assignments)

2 = Observed   3 = Beyond expectations ☺

Today's goal _____   Points earned today _____

[Designated adult] Notes:

_____

_____

Designated adult's signature

Parent notes:

_____

Parent's signature

> Question from the Tour Guides: What strategies and mechanisms would you use for monitoring Daryl's progress?

DOCUMENTATION

Documenting our work with student clients is yet another time consuming, though important, task. Maintaining a session-to-session record helps professionals provide continuity, identify themes, remain accountable, and monitor progress. We outlined the commonly used SOAP structure in Chapter 12 of *Counseling Children and Adolescents in Schools*. In this tour of the *Practice and Application Guide*, we provide an opportunity for you to evaluate comments that might appear in case notes and develop notes for Daryl.

Efficiency and time management are prominent values for school-based professional helpers, even in terms of documentation. Thus, we encourage you to develop strategies for "writing less and documenting more" with precision and focus. Additionally, we encourage you to write as if your notes were going to be printed on the front page of your city's newspaper.

What do you think of the following documentation entries?

- John came in, and we chatted awhile.
- She was messier than usual.
- She complained about feeling uneasy and strange. We talked about ways to deal with her uncomfortable feelings.
- Todd said that his teacher, Mr. Bell, is impossible to deal with and that he often yells at the kids.
- She has set unrealistic goals for herself, and I tried to convince her that she should focus on what she can achieve.
- Ann played, drew some pictures, and then said she had to leave.

You probably noticed that the entries include vague generalities that are, essentially, meaningless. A few of the references are pejorative. What did Ann play? What did she draw? What prompted her decision to leave? How long is *awhile*? What is an *unrealistic goal*?

When preparing, reviewing, and evaluating documentation, strive for the following qualities:

- Precise
- Parsimonious
- Promptly prepared
- Professional
- Prudent
- Protected to ensure confidentiality

Develop a SOAP note for your first session with Daryl.

S: (Subjective—Summary of what he said):

_____

_____

_____

_____

O: (Objective—Your observations):

_____

_____

_____

_____

A: (Assessment—Your assessment of the student's situation and progress toward goals):

_____

_____

_____

_____

P: (Plan—Homework given, plans for subsequent sessions, tasks prior to the next session):

_____

_____

_____

_____

Your conceptualization and SOAP notes should be logically connected and consistent. Essentially, you are recording a nonfiction story.

Your Second Session With Daryl

Following Daryl's request, you wait in your office for him. You did, however, ask his teacher to remind him about the appointment. Daryl arrives just 5 minutes after the appointed time. What thoughts did you have while you waited? When he arrives, what will you say? How will you begin your session? We invite you to introduce the dialogue that is transcribed next.

You:

_____

_____

Daryl:

_____

_____

You:

_____

_____

Daryl:

_____

_____

You: I'm wondering what thoughts you had last week when you left my office.

Daryl: I don't know—Don't know that I had any thoughts. It was okay, I guess.

You: Sometimes students think about things when they leave, so I like to ask. I gave you a homework assignment last week. I asked you to pay attention to the times—

Daryl: Well, Wednesday and Thursday weren't good days. I was more stressed than usual. I didn't get to school until after lunch on Wednesday and then I just didn't come on Thursday.

You: Okay. Wednesday and Thursday were kind of rough. What about the other days?

Daryl: Friday was a good day. I didn't have any classes until 11:00, and I felt good enough to get to school before I needed to be in class.

You: How did you get that to happen?

Daryl: I got to sleep earlier Thursday night so I felt better when I woke up.

You: You went to bed earlier, rested well, and felt good this morning. [Pause] Last week I asked you how you will know when our work together has been helpful. I used your ideas to create a plan for us. I wrote a few ideas for goals—but you may have other ideas today. This is just a place for us to begin. We'll finish it together. You said that you would be catching up on your homework. For a goal, I wrote, "I will work with each of my teachers to figure out a plan so I can catch up." How does that fit for you?

Daryl: That's okay I guess.

You: You guess. You aren't sure about being able to reach that goal.

Daryl: I don't know about Mr. Thompson and Ms. Sanchez. We don't get along so well.

You: Okay. Is that goal something you still would like to work toward?

Daryl: I need to catch up if I'm going to stay in school.

You: Okay, we'll figure out strategies for catching up. I have two other goals I'd like you to consider.

Document your second session with Daryl, assuming that the session went well and that you were fully satisfied with the work you did and Daryl's responses.

S: (Subjective—Summary of what he said):

_____

_____

_____

_____

O: (Objective—Your observations):

_____

_____

_____

_____

_____

A: (Assessment—Your assessment of the student's situation and progress toward goals):

_____

_____

_____

_____

P: (Plan—Homework given, plans for subsequent sessions, tasks prior to the next session):

_____

_____

_____

_____

Tours 4 and 5 have been dense, less defined, and somewhat ambiguous. We've invited you to begin activities that have not been completed and likely won't ever be "complete." We've identified challenges. We've provided frameworks for time intensive tasks that must be completed even though they don't demand your attention with knocks, rings, and e-mail. What's going on with you now? Please take a few moments to journal your thoughts and feelings.

TOUR 6

Consolidation

Celebrating the Journey and Preparing to Go Our Separate Ways

Learning Objectives

- Refine clarity of your essential beliefs
- Personalize authenticity, respect, empathy, and engagement
- Prepare for self-directed tours

Tour Guide Note: As we begin this tour, we are reminded of the closing stage in group counseling. Thus, we titled the tour "Consolidation." Just as group members often approach the final phases of group with ambivalence, and sometimes reluctance, we have encountered that same experience when finishing *Counseling Children and Adolescents in Schools* and this *Practice and Application Guide*. On one hand, we are glad our immediate task is almost over. On the other, we continue to think of things to include. The task has been a major line on our planners; its completion is also a loss. Undoubtedly you, the readers, have a degree of ambivalence as you near the end of this course or program requirement.

During our final tour, we encourage you to participate in thoughtful and reflective activities designed to consolidate your thinking about your work and multiple roles as a professional helper in schools and to document those thoughts. These activities are not intended to be a final statement. In fact, we predict that you will adopt different beliefs and values as you engage in your profession, work in various settings, and encounter a variety of students. We hope we have challenged and inspired you to intentionally keep that journey alive!

As we anticipated the directions and topics for this *Guide*, we prepared a "map" to achieve and communicate our own philosophical clarity about skill development, theory building, application, and professional helpers' work in schools (see Figure 6.1).

As shown in the graphic representation, basic skills are central yet integrally connected to the other circles. To sound basic skills, we added advanced facilitation skills. Theories in isolation were added (with references to *Counseling Children and Adolescents in Schools* and your other counseling theories texts) and considered in the context of our work in schools. We emphasized the importance of respecting diversity—of cultural groups and individuals within those groups. We explored conditions

Figure 6.1 Conceptualization of Skill Acquisition and Professional Development

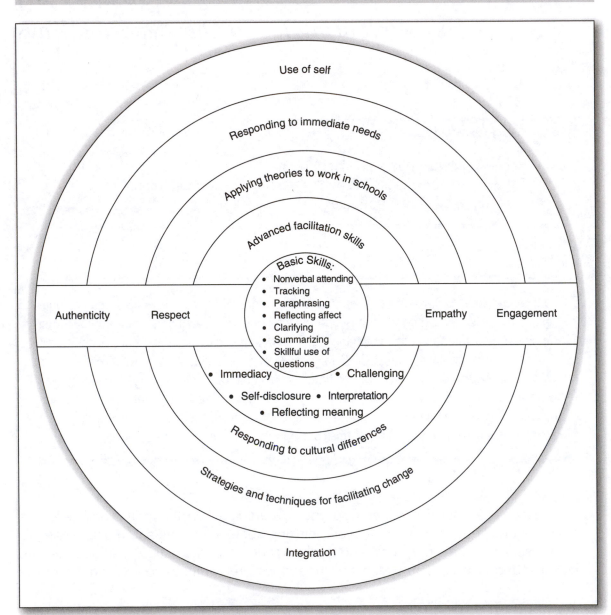

and strategies for effecting change. An overview of areas to consider and procedures to follow when responding to immediate needs of students as well as school communities was provided in *Counseling Children and Adolescents in Schools.*

Your voice (at least your thoughts and words) became more prominent on Tours 4 and 5. We invited you to draw many of your own conclusions related to counseling children and adolescents in schools. We also encouraged you to engage in the conceptualization process for a student client with whom you might work. Our emphasis broadened because you are becoming "the person of the school counselor" or "the person of the school psychologist," the unifying element to all the work *you* will do in schools. In our conceptual understanding of professional development, authenticity, respect, empathy, and engagement—which we view as critical in all professional helping contexts—transcend each layer of skill progression. Our overall goal for Tours 4, 5, and 6 is to help you maximize and professionalize your unique healing qualities to help while personalizing the many skills, theories, and interventions you have learned.

As you prepare to conclude this portion of your career journey, what meanings do authenticity, respect, empathy, and engagement have for you? How do you know when you are becoming inauthentic or disrespectful? How do you know when you are empathic? How do you recognize engagement?

We have come to the outer ring of Figure 6.1, but your professional journey is just beginning. We visualize many arrows pointing away from this outer ring. Each arrow represents a preservice professional who has journeyed with us through this series of guided tours. You will continue to grow with the support of other "tour guides" as well as through many self-guided tours. Where will your professional preparation take you and where will you take it? We invite you to ponder those questions for a few moments. Undoubtedly, you are feeling stressed by end-of-an-academic-term requirements, yet we encourage you to devote time for journaling your reactions.

PACKING TO EMBARK ON YOUR NEXT TOUR

At the conclusion of Tour 4, we encouraged you to begin "packing" with a system for organization. On this tour, we will suggest strategies for that process. Some may fit for you, others will not. You're the consumer and the sojourner!

Throughout *Counseling Children and Adolescents in Schools* and this *Guide*, we have asked about your thoughts, beliefs, values, and so forth. Just as possessions get lost or forgotten when they're simply boxed and stashed when we travel, so ideas, strategies, possibilities, and plans are easily forgotten. We encourage you to formulate as much clarity as possible about your beliefs related to your work as a professional helper, and to "pack" the results so they are not lost. The following activities are designed to help you do that.

Imagine that you were required to distill all of your beliefs and values that pertain to professional helping into 10 statements, each of which is explained in a short paragraph (Recommended or modeled by Conyne, 1997; Dolliver, 1991; Fontaine & Hammond, 1994; and Magnuson, 2000a).

"Maxims" that I (S.M.) have composed at various junctures in my career include the following:

- I cannot possibly know enough to effectively and competently help all students in my school. Thus, it is imperative that I commit to an agenda of learning and supervision that will extend throughout my professional lifespan. I must also implicitly invite students to teach me how to work most effectively with them.
- The most critical thing I can offer students is a relationship that enables them to find solutions to problems, achieve resolution, and grow. I must earn the right to intervene in a child's life by investing ample time to ensure that the student and I both experience engagement.
- I am responsible to all of the children in my school. In fact, I may be the only advocate that some students have. If I solely consider outward appearances, some will be dirty, different, and unlovely. These children need my loyalty! I cannot let them down!
- Counseling is a science and an art. As with any art form, I must mold, blend, and synthesize basic principles, theories, strategies, and interventions with my personality, philosophy of counseling, ethical standards, and approaches. Within that framework, I can more effectively appreciate and respond to the unique needs and personality of each student and adult in my school.
- Mine is a profession of privilege. If I fail to communicate respect and unconditional positive regard to students and adults in my school, I fall short of living in accordance with the values I claim to prize. Although I believe integrity and authenticity are journeys rather than destinations, I must monitor and assess the extent to which I remain committed to those journeys on a moment-to-moment basis.

Now, it's your turn. As you begin the process, claim it as yours! What will you call your list? Maxims? Ideas? Reflections? Professional Declaration? Aphorisms? Think about your role as a school psychologist or school counselor. You might focus on individual counseling or your comprehensive role as a professional helper. For now, don't limit yourself to a finite number of statements. Just compose statements that are compelling for you at this moment in time. Regardless of the format and parameters you choose, we challenge you to begin this activity, revisit it in a few days before temporarily finalizing it, and revisit it from time to time to (a) ground yourself and (b) revise the document to reflect your professional and personal growth. We also encourage you to share your statements with peers.

Tour Guide Note: Graphic representations such as Figure 6.1 schematically help many professional helpers achieve clarity. For suggestions and examples access Magnuson (2000b) or Wubbolding (2011, p. 48).

THE PERSON OF THE SCHOOL-BASED PROFESSIONAL HELPER: THAT'S YOU!

Garry Landreth (2002) offered a format that you may prefer, or an additional activity you might like to do. Based on his experiences, he composed a list of principles for relationships with children using "I am (or am not) _____; therefore I will (or will not) _____" format. As you read selected examples of Landreth's principles, think about similar statements you might write.

- I am not all knowing. Therefore, I will not even attempt to be.
- I need to be loved. Therefore, I will be open to loving children.
- I know so little about the complex intricacies of childhood. Therefore, I will allow children to teach me.
- I learn best and am impacted most by my personal struggles. Therefore, I will join with children in their struggles.
- I sometimes need a refuge. Therefore, I will provide a refuge for children.
- I like it when I am fully accepted as the person I am. Therefore, I will strive to experience and appreciate the person of the child.
- I make mistakes. They are a declaration of the way I am—human and fallible. Therefore, I will be tolerant of the humanness of children.
- It feels good to be an authority, to provide answers. Therefore, I will need to work hard to protect children from me!
- I cannot make children's hurts and fears and frustrations and disappointments go away. Therefore, I will soften the blow.
- I experience fear when I am vulnerable. Therefore, I will with kindness, gentleness, and tenderness touch the inner world of the vulnerable child. (pp. 5–7)

Again, it's your turn. With which statements do you resonate? Which seem more relevant to your work as a school-based professional helper? Which seem unrealistic? More important, what would you write? Even writing four or five statements will mark the beginning of possibilities for you.

Our professional demeanor and posture cannot be separated from our psychological health and personal growth. What does that mean to you? Many professional helpers participate in individual or group counseling. Personal growth is sometimes included in individual or group supervision. Challenging personal growth literature is also available.

As you proceed on your career journey, we hope you will guard against compromising your own health—physically and psychologically. Attend to indicators that you are approaching exhaustion, that you need a break, that your life is out of balance, that your energy and interest are fading, and that your patience with yourself and others is diminishing. Clarify your priorities in personal and professional categories, so you can compare those priorities to your planning calendar. We encourage you to make a commitment to yourself regarding your personal growth in ways that are effective for you.

Imagine sitting in your office at the end of a day when you encountered a series of unscheduled responsibilities, in addition to those several you had planned. A parent was waiting when you arrived at school to tell you that her son's grandfather, with whom they were particularly close, had been transferred to a hospice unit. They hoped you would be able to check on the boys from time to time. There was also a note from your colleague; cultures confirmed that he had strep throat. A guest speaker came for your weekly Let's Talk about Careers meeting. You hosted the Yarn

Club during first block lunch. Key Club met during second block lunch. Two students came to your office for individual appointments. You facilitated a study skills group and conducted lessons on anger management in three classes. You are hungry, and it's nearly time for dinner.

Your desk is—essentially—a mess. You have three phone call messages, and you haven't even looked at e-mail. The building is empty. You have an opportunity to catch up with e-mail and phone messages, clean your desk, and get organized for tomorrow. But what about dinner? And, by the way, your throat is feeling sore.

How will you manage the tension between your personal life, even having dinner, and the tendency to think, "I'm the only one that can do this. If I don't do this, it won't get done. If I don't do it now, I'll be even further behind tomorrow"?

_____

_____

_____

_____

How does your internal wisdom communicate messages such as, "You need to take a break?" (e.g., some people begin to feel tense in their shoulders or across their forehead.)

_____

_____

_____

What relaxation strategies have been most effective for you as a graduate student?

_____

_____

_____

To what self-care activities are you committed?

_____

_____

_____

INTEGRATION

For a moment or two, reflect on the theories that make the most sense for you, statements you wrote for the previous two activities, and your growth this semester. How do aspects of those various elements fit together? How might your fundamental beliefs contradict aspects of your preferred theories? Allow these tensions to emerge and then embrace them! With this level of intentionality, you will find ways to use theories and your personal therapeutic assets without compromising either.

OUR FINAL WORDS ABOUT ALL THE WORDS!

As we near the time when we say "farewell," we checked our resources to ensure that we had fulfilled tasks associated with groups' consolidation. We have tried to normalize ambivalence. We hope we have reinforced the growth you experienced as we journeyed together. We have endeavored to share strategies that will contribute to your ongoing professional maturity. We've addressed integration with a fair amount of thoroughness. But how do we facilitate closure when we want you to continue your work without us? And how will we be able to evaluate the effectiveness of our work with you? As you unpack resources and experiences we've provided, perhaps you'll let us know about that!

And with that invitation, we extend our best wishes for long, successful, and fulfilling career journeys. Bon voyage!

• Sandy, Robyn, and Linda

References

Bankart, C. P. (1997). *Talking cures: A history of Western and Eastern psychotherapies*. Pacific Grove, CA: Brooks Cole.

Beale, A. (1993). Contemporary counseling approaches: A review for the practitioner. *School Counselor, 40*(4), 282–286.

Berman, P. S. (2010). *Case conceptualization and treatment planning: Integrating theory with clinical practice*. Thousand Oaks, CA: Sage.

Combs, A. W., & Gonzalez, D. M. (1994). *Helping relationships: Basic concepts for the helping professions* (4th ed.). Boston: Allyn & Bacon.

Conyne, R. K. (1997). Group work ideas I have made aphoristic (for me). *Journal for Specialists in Group Work, 22,* 149–156.

Cowles, J. (1997). Lessons from "The Little Prince": Therapeutic relationships with children. *Professional School Counseling, 1,* 57–60.

Crone, D. A., Horner, R. H., & Hawken, L. S. (2010). *Responding to problem behaviors in schools: The behavioral education program* (2nd ed.). New York: Guilford.

D'Andrea, M., Daniels, J., & Heck, R. (1991). Evaluating the impact of multicultural counseling training. *Journal of Counseling and Development, 70,* 149–150.

Dolliver, R. H. (1991). The eighteen ideas which most influence my therapy. *Psychotherapy, 28,* 507–514.

Dreikurs, R. (1967). *Psychodynamics, psychotherapy, and counseling*. Chicago: Alfred Adler Institute.

Elliott, R., Shapiro, D. A., Firth-Cozens, J., Stiles, W. B., Hardy, G. E., & Llewelyn, S. P. (1994). Comprehensive process analysis of insight events in cognitive-behavioral and psychodynamic-interpersonal psychotherapies. *Journal of Counseling Psychology, 41,* 449–463.

Eysenck, H. J. (1970). A mish-mash of theories. *International Journal of Psychiatry, 2,* 140–146.

Faber, A., & Mazlish, E. (1992*). How to talk so kids will listen and listen so kids will talk*. New York: Avon.

Fontaine, J. H., & Hammond, N. L. (1994). Twenty counseling maxims. *Journal of Counseling and Development, 73,* 223–226.

Gladding, S. T. (2006). *The counseling dictionary: Concise definitions of frequently used terms* (2nd ed.). Upper Saddle River, NJ: Prentice Hall.

Gordon, T. (1970). *Parent effectiveness training: A "no-lose" program for raising responsible children*. New York: Peter H. Wyden.

Gordon, T. (1974). *T. E. T.: Teacher effectiveness training*. New York: Peter H. Wyden.

Greenberg, L. S., Watson, J. C., Elliott, R., & Bohart, A. C. (2001). Empathy. *Psychotherapy, 38,* 380–384.

Halbur, D. A., & Halbur, K. V. (2011). *Developing your theoretical orientation in counseling and psychotherapy* (2nd ed.). Upper Saddle River, NJ: Pearson.

Highlen, P. S., & Hill, C. E. (1984). Factors affecting client change in individual counseling: Current status and theoretical speculations. In S. D. Brown & R. W. Lent (Eds.), *Handbook of counseling psychology* (pp. 334–396). New York: Wiley.

Hill, C. E. (2004). *Helping skills: Facilitating exploration, insight, and action* (2nd ed.). Washington, DC: American Psychological Association.

Lambert, M., & Barley, D. E. (2001). Research summary on the therapeutic relationship and psychotherapy outcome. *Psychotherapy: Theory, Research, Practice, and Training, 38,* 357–361.

Landreth, G. L. (2002). *Play therapy: The art of the relationship* (2nd ed.). New York: Brunner-Routledge.

Magnuson, S. (2000a). Clarifying epistemology with statements of fundamental professional assumptions. *Journal of Humanistic Education and Development, 38,* 252–256.

Magnuson, S. (2000b). Clarifying a professional paradigm with a schematic model. *Guidance and Counselling, 16*(1), 9–11.

Maslow, A. H. (1965). A philosophy of psychology: The need of a mature science of human nature. In F. T. Severin (Ed.), *Humanistic viewpoints in psychology: A book of readings* (pp. 17–33). New York: McGraw-Hill.

Mennuti, R. B., Freeman, A., & Christner, R. W. (2006). *Cognitive-behavioral interventions in educational settings: A handbook for practice.* New York: Routledge.

Metcalf, L. (2008). *Counseling toward solutions: A practical solution focused program for working with students, teachers, and parents* (2nd ed.). San Francisco, CA: Jossey-Bass.

Murphy, V. B., & Christner, R. W. (2006). A cognitive-behavioral case conceptualization approach for working with children and adolescents. In R. B. Mennuti, A. Freeman, & R. W. Christner (Eds.), *Cognitive-behavioral interventions in educational settings: A handbook for practice* (pp. 37–62). New York: Routledge.

Neufeldt, S. A., Iversen, J. N., & Juntunen, C. L. (1995). *Supervision strategies for the first practicum.* Alexandria, VA: American Counseling Association.

Rogers, C. R. (1957). The necessary and sufficient conditions of therapeutic personality change. *Journal of Consulting and Clinical Psychology, 21,* 95–103.

Rogers, C. R. (1961). *On becoming a person.* Boston: Houghton Mifflin.

Rogers, C. R. (1980). *A way of being.* Boston: Houghton Mifflin.

Schon, D. A. (1987). *Educating the reflective practitioner.* San Francisco: Jossey-Bass.

Severin, F. T. (Ed.). (1965). *Humanistic viewpoints in psychology: A book of readings.* New York: McGraw-Hill.

Sklare, G., Portes, P., & Splete, H. (1985). Developing questioning effectiveness in counseling. *Counselor Education and Supervision, 25,* 12–20.

Smyth, J. (1989). Developing and sustaining critical reflection in teacher education. *Journal of Teacher Education, 40,* 2–9.

Stickel, S. A., & Trimmer, K. J. (1994). Knowing in action: A first-year counselor's process of reflection. *Elementary School Guidance & Counseling, 29,* 102–109.

Van Velsor, P. (2004). Revisiting basic counseling skills with children. *Journal of Counseling and Development, 82,* 313–318.

Wampold, B. E. (2001). *The great psychotherapy debate: Models, methods, and findings.* Mahwah, NJ: Erlbaum.

Watts, R. E. (1993). Developing a personal theory of counseling: A brief guide for students. *TCA Journal, 21*(1), 103–104.

Watzlawick, P., Beavin, J., & Jackson, D. (1967). *Pragmatics of human behavior: A study of interactional patterns, pathologies, and paradoxes.* New York: W. W. Norton.

Welch, I. D. (1998). *The path of psychotherapy: Matters of the heart.* Pacific Grove, CA: Brooks Cole.

Welch, I. D., & Gonzalez, D. M. (1999). *The process of counseling and psychotherapy: Matters of skill.* Pacific Grove, CA: Brooks Cole.

Wubbolding, R. E. (2011). *Reality therapy.* Washington, DC: American Psychological Association.

About the Authors

Sandy Magnuson received her master's degree in elementary school counseling at Southwest Missouri State University in 1983. Her doctoral work in counselor education was completed at the University of Alabama. After teaching in counselor education programs in Alabama, Texas, and Colorado, Dr. Magnuson returned to the wonderful world of elementary school counseling at University Schools in Greeley, Colorado. She retired in 2010. During her career as a counselor educator and school counselor, she was committed to active participation in school counseling organizations and her own continuing education and supervision. She also conducted research related to development of counselors across the professional life span and supervision of counselors. Dr. Magnuson has authored over 60 articles that have been published in professional journals. She is a Licensed Professional Counselor and Licensed School Counselor in the state of Colorado as well as an approved supervisor and clinical member of the American Association for Marriage and Family Therapy.

Robyn S. Hess is a professor and chair of the Department of School Psychology at the University of Northern Colorado. She earned her doctorate in school psychology in 1993 and her MS in counseling psychology in 1987. Dr. Hess blends her experiences as a counselor, school psychologist, and academician to provide a scholarly yet practical approach to understanding counseling and mental health promotion within schools. She has published both nationally and internationally in the areas of culturally responsive assessment and intervention strategies, coping and stress in children and adolescents, and school completion among high risk youth. Her teaching assignments over the last 6 years have included introductory counseling practica and children's mental health. Dr. Hess is a licensed psychologist and school psychologist in the state of Colorado. She is also board certified in the area of school psychology by the American Board of Professional Psychology.

Linda Beeler currently serves as core faculty in the School Counseling specialization for the Department of Counselor Education at Capella University. She earned her PhD in counselor education and supervision from the University of Northern Colorado in 2001 and began working in the public schools at that time. She has carved a niche for herself in working with high needs and at risk youth and has also been actively involved in crisis intervention work in the schools. An additional area of focus for Dr. Beeler is in the supervision of current school counselors and school counselors-in-training. She holds the Approved Clinical Supervisor credential.

SAGE Research Methods Online
The essential tool for researchers

Sign up now at www.sagepub.com/srmo for more information.

An expert research tool

- An **expertly designed taxonomy** with more than 1,400 unique terms for social and behavioral science research methods

- **Visual and hierarchical search tools** to help you discover material and link to related methods

- Easy-to-use navigation tools
- Content organized by complexity
- Tools for citing, printing, and downloading content with ease
- Regularly updated content and features

A wealth of essential content

- The most comprehensive picture of quantitative, qualitative, and mixed methods available today

- More than **100,000 pages of SAGE book and reference material** on research methods as well as editorially selected material from SAGE journals

- More than **600 books** available in their entirety online

Launching 2011!

⑤SAGE research methods online